Exposing Satan's Devices Workbook

by
R. S. "Bud" Miller, D.D.
Publisher
Betty Miller, D.M.
Author
www.BibleResources.org

Overcoming Life Series

Christ Unlimited — P.O. Box 850 — Dewey, AZ 86327   USA

Unless otherwise indicated, all Scripture quotations are taken from the King James Version of the Holy Bible (KJV).

Overcoming Life Series:

Exposing Satan's Devices Workbook

ISBN 1-57149-009-4

Copyright (C) 1993-2013

R. S. "Bud" and Betty Miller

P.O. Box 850

Dewey, Arizona 86327 USA

www.BibleResources.org

Published by

Christ Unlimited Publishing

P. O. Box 850

Dewey, Arizona 86327

Publisher: Pastor R. S. "Bud" Miller

Contents

Christ Unlimited — P.O. Box 850 — Dewey, AZ 86327   USA

Personal Introduction

A lack of education will not hinder anyone from taking this course, and a doctor's degree will not help. However, one requirement that is necessary for this course to benefit the student is a total commitment to God. The Holy Spirit is our teacher, and we can learn if we come to God as little children. Being hungry to know God is a necessary prerequisite in order for this course to be of help.

If any of us are to receive truth, we must seek God, who is truth, with our whole hearts. We must seek Jesus first, then the knowledge of His Word will be revealed to us. Therefore, I want to emphasize once again the need to become as "a little child" in our approach to learning God's Word (Matthew 18:1-4; Jeremiah 29:13).

We need to come humbly before God, asking Him to remove any "know-it-all" attitudes, in order to be teachable. By laying down everything we thought we knew, we give God a chance to correct things we have believed that were wrong. Then we can begin to live the overcoming lives that God intended for His children to experience.

This course, the Overcoming Life Series, is made up of nine books and workbooks taken from our first published book, How To Overcome Through the Christ Unlimited. That book, given to us under the anointing of the Holy Spirit, covers most of the basic things a Christian needs to know to get started on a victorious, overcoming walk with the Lord.

We have purposely kept this course simple for the average Christian who needs help in understanding how to study the Word and how to sort out principles and concepts when he, or she, reads the Bible; however, it also is for the seminary student. In addition, it is designed for students who desire to use it as a correspondence course. They can learn from it, even if they are totally alone and without a human teacher. The Holy Spirit always is there to teach us as we study about His Word.

On the other hand, groups with a teacher, or moderator, also can use this course to advantage. Our prayer is that, however this course is taken, each student will complete it a different person and be conformed more into the image of Christ our Lord.

Bud and Betty Miller

Exposing Satan's Devices Workbook

Section One

"Defining Our Enemy"

Christ Unlimited — P.O. Box 850 — Dewey, AZ 86327   USA

Exposing Satan's Devices Workbook
Section One: "Defining Our Enemy"
Expository Introduction

[**Author's Note:** This <u>Overcoming Life Series Workbook</u> is based on the book <u>Exposing Satan's Devices</u>. There are nine books and workbooks in this series. This workbook has six sections, and each section contains material in addition to the book. All scripture references that answer the questions in the lessons have been given. Answers are provided at the end of the workbook and do not have to be the exact wording in many cases. We ask students not to look at the answers until the questions have been answered. This is <u>not</u> a test, but an expository lesson to enhance study of the Bible.]

Second Corinthians 2:11 tells us that we are not to be ignorant of Satan's devices, lest he should get an advantage over us. He tries to get us to ignore him and think he does not exist. However, the Word of God has much to say on the subject of the devil. In fact, the words <u>Satan, devil, Lucifer,</u> along with <u>hell</u> are mentioned more than 280 times in the Bible.

Two of the most important truths a Christian should know are <u>who the enemy is</u> and <u>what his tactics are</u>. We are not to <u>ignore</u> the devil or to be <u>ignorant of</u> him, but we are to <u>resist</u> him, according to James 4:7.

In natural warfare, an army is trained in the latest techniques of how to overcome the enemy's battle plans and tactics. Soldiers are taught how to recognize the enemy, even in camouflage. It is much more necessary to know these things in spiritual warfare. **Hosea 4:6** says that God's people are destroyed for <u>lack of knowledge</u>.

Christ Unlimited — P.O. Box 850 — Dewey, AZ 86327   USA

Today, many Christians are being destroyed because they do not know about their number-one enemy. Satan is stealing their inheritances: their blessings under the Blood Covenant that Jesus bought for them. **Acts 26:18** says that we have to understand the enemy in order to know our inheritances. Until Satan is bound in the pit (**Rev. 20:1-3**), we must know the authority Jesus gave us over him and the weapons provided by the Father with which to fight him.

The word <u>satan</u> comes from a Hebrew word meaning "adversary, enemy, or accuser," so when we say, "Satan", we really are saying, "You adversary, you accuser, or you enemy, listen to what I say to you in the name of Jesus!" However, in the Bible, he is called by at least twenty-six "labels" or descriptions of what he is or does.

In the lesson for this section, references are given from the Word of God to enable the student to look up these names, which also describe his ways and character. <u>Satan</u> is a "label" or a descriptive term, as are most of the others. His real name, as originally he was called in Scripture, is <u>Lucifer</u> (Isaiah 14:12).

What God saw fit to reveal to us about the origin of Satan is recorded in **Ezekiel 28:12-19**. According to these scriptures, he was created by God as a perfect, beautiful cherub (the <u>cherubim</u> are higher forms of heavenly beings in the angelic order) with no sin in him, apparently having a free will. He chose to walk in rebellion, and from that day on, iniquity was found in him (**Ezekiel 28:15**).

Christ Unlimited — P.O. Box 850 — Dewey, AZ 86327   USA

Why did he sin? What could have caused a perfect being to think he could be above God? **Isaiah 14:12-15** tells us that it was pride and self-will that led Lucifer to set himself against God. Isaiah wrote that Lucifer declared, "I will," five times in opposition to God.

Man's primary sin today is the same as Satan's: pride, self-will, and rebellion. If we insist on our wills instead of God's in any area, we are in rebellion against God.

In his battle to overthrow the Lord God Almighty, Satan corrupted a third of the heavenly angels. They were thrown out of Heaven with him (**Rev. 12:4**). Since the creation of Adam and Eve, Satan has corrupted many billions of human beings. All sin and anti-Christ thoughts, actions, attitudes, and systems come from Lucifer's first act of rebellion.

God Did Not Create Evil

God never intended for evil to exist. It is simply the opposite of good. Every good and perfect gift comes from God, and all evil proceeds from Satan and sin. God did not create evil by making something bad. He gave mankind the right to choose good or evil in order to gain children who would voluntarily love and serve Him.

God only created the <u>situation</u> in which evil is allowed to exist. That was necessary in order to have circumstances in which mankind could choose God of their own free wills. However, God did not allow Satan to continue to exist on earth without providing the remedy and the power to overcome him.

To live the overcoming life, we must understand that <u>every good and perfect gift</u> comes from God above, and <u>all</u> evil comes from Satan. Satan is referred to as the "god of this world" (**2 Cor. 4:4**), which means the ruler of all world systems, the "god of this world order."

When Adam failed his responsibilities and allowed Eve to eat the forbidden fruit (even joining her in disobedience), the dominion (rule) over the earth given to him by God (**Gen. 1:26-28**) then passed to the adversary, who in essence, cheated Adam out of it.

But when Jesus died on the cross, He defeated the works of Satan (**1 John 3:8**), which was the main purpose for which He had come to earth. He had to defeat the works of Satan in order to redeem man. Man's downfall was one of Satan's biggest "works".

On the cross, Jesus stripped Satan of his authority (**Col. 2:14**). Then, when Jesus returned to Heaven to sit at the right hand of the Father, He delegated His authority to His Body, the Church. However, most Christians do not realize the authority that they possess, so we do not see a full manifestation of Christ's defeat over the enemy. Therefore, Satan and his troops have a "hey-day".

At the point of Satan's defeat at the cross, Jesus gave us the legal right to have victory over the enemy. We do not have to fear the devil, although he is in the earth. Before the cross, Satan also had access to Heaven, walking up and down and in and out before the throne of God (Job 1:6,7). Today, he no longer has access to Heaven, but he continues to roam the earth seeking whom he may devour (1 Peter 5:8).

Walking after the flesh (after Satan) causes "the law of sin and death" to work in human lives (Rom. 8:2-6), paving the way for sickness and disease — even death. However, God did not originate sickness and disease, and He does not use it to "teach us a lesson," as some believe.

We Have Power Over the Enemy

It is not God's will that anyone should be sick, but rather that we all should be in good health and prosper (3 John 2; 1 Thess. 5:23). Sickness is from the devil, and we should resist it just as we do any temptation of the enemy. The "door" through which infirmities come upon us may be generational sin (a chain of iniquity from our forefathers), past sins of our own, ignorance of our rights in Christ through the cross, or simply an attack by the enemy.

The point is: Reject the infirmity. Infirmities are from the devil, and we do not have to receive them. We need to stand in obedience to the Word of God and be healed (Isa. 53:5; 1 Pet. 2:24; James 5:14,15).

In the Holy Spirit, we have power over anything the devil can bring against us, even the spirit of death. We even have the power as Christians to lay hands on one who has died prematurely and command them to be raised from the dead. The problem is that few of us have that kind of faith, even though we have been given the authority (Matthew 10:8; John 14:12).

As Christians, we need to learn how to use the Word of God against sickness and attacks from the enemy. James 4:7 says that if we resist the devil, he <u>will</u> flee. However, it takes spiritual tools and effort to resist him. Those tools include such things as fasting, prayer, and travailing in the spirit. The devil should be running from us instead of the other way around. Jesus already has overcome the world (John 16:33) and has defeated the devil for us (1 John 3:8).

How, then, can we recognize the works of the enemy? We do this first of all by studying the Bible to find out what God's will is and what He has already said about various situations. If we do that, in times of attack, the Word itself will rise up out of our spirits and flow out of our mouths to defeat the enemy. The Word acts like a bomb that destroys the enemy.

Ephesians 5:11-13 says:

And have no fellowship with the unfruitful works of darkness, but rather reprove them. For it is a shame even to speak of those things which are done of them in secret. But all things that are reproved are made manifest by the light: for whatsoever doth make manifest is light.

Christ Unlimited — P.O. Box 850 — Dewey, AZ 86327   USA

We should never study books on the occult and satanism in order to learn about the enemy. That puts us on his territory and gives him a certain amount of power over us. Those books are snares. The Bible tells us all we need to know about the enemy. Many people who have studied this literature out of curiosity or even with right motives have come under the spell of witchcraft and fear.

If Christians possess any objects related to witchcraft or idols in their homes or other places, they should get rid of them immediately.

Most of the time, new Christians need advice and counsel from older Christians to be able to discern good and evil (Heb. 5:13,14). Younger ones should submit to this counsel and advice, thus sparing themselves a lot of heartache, even if they do not always understand the spiritual implications attached to these objects. The Bible declares that a curse comes connected with idols and objects that are an abomination to God (Deuteronomy 7:25,26).

The enemy wants us to ignore him and believe he does not exist. But there is no place in the Bible that says, "Ignore the devil, and he will go away." James 4:7 says to resist him, and he will flee. Satan wants us to fear him and blame God for our problems. 1 Peter 5:8 admonishes us to:

Be sober, be vigilant: because your adversary the devil, as a roaring lion, walketh about, seeking whom he may devour.

Christ Unlimited — P.O. Box 850 — Dewey, AZ 86327   USA

The devil tries to make us think he is bigger than us and has more power. Yet a child who knows Jesus and how to use His name can defeat the devil. The Bible says that God did not give us a spirit of fear (**2 Tim. 1:7**). Instead, He has given us love, power, and a sound mind.

Satan tries to convince Christians that they have no power over him, but that he is the one who has power over them. However, the truth is that the only power Satan ever has over Christians is through deception. If we are convinced that circumstances are God's fault, then we will not bother to resist the devil.

Deception comes through not knowing the Word of God. However, by being a hearer and a doer of the Word, we are able to overcome deception in our lives (**James 1:22**). **Revelation 12:9-11** says that Satan deceives the whole world. He even uses deceived brethren (Christians into error) to deceive the hearts of the simple (**Rom. 16:17,18**). Defining the enemy, therefore, becomes of prime importance to our overcoming him.

Christ Unlimited — P.O. Box 850 — Dewey, AZ 86327   USA

Lesson for Section One

[Author's Note: Please read Chapter 1 in <u>Exposing Satan's Devices</u>, and the preceding expository introduction before beginning this lesson.]

I.   Satan's Name and Origin

A. <u>Satan</u> comes from a Hebrew word meaning:

1. _____

References:

Job 1:6; John 13:27; Acts 5:3, 26:18; Romans 16:20

2. Other names by which he is called in the Bible are:

a. _____ Revelation 9:11

b. _____ Revelation 12:10

c. _____ 1 Peter 5:8

d. _____ Revelation 9:11

e. _____ Revelation 9:11

f. _____ Mark 3:22

g. _____ 2 Corinthians 6:15

h. _____ Jeremiah 51:25
                                                1 Corinthians 10:10

Christ Unlimited — P.O. Box 850 — Dewey, AZ 86327   USA

i. _____ Matthew 4:1; Luke 4:2,6

j. _____ Matthew 13:39

k. _____ John 8:44

l. _____ Revelation 12:3

m. _____ John 10:10

n. _____ Isaiah 14:12

o. _____ Ezekiel 28:12-15

p. _____ John 8:44

q. _____ Revelation 12:9, 20:2

r. _____ John 12:31, 14:30

s. _____ Matthew 12:24

t. _____ Ephesians 2:2

u. _____ Genesis 3:4,14
                            2 Corinthians 11:3

v. _____ Ephesians 2:2

w. _____ Matthew 4:3; 1 Thessolonians 3:5

Christ Unlimited — P.O. Box 850 — Dewey, AZ 86327   USA

x. _____ 2 Corinthians 4:4

y. _____ Matthew 13:19, 38

z. _____ John 10:10-12

aa. _____ 1 John 4:3

bb. _____ Revelation 13:1

B. Where did Satan come from? _____

Son of man, take up a lamentation upon the king of Tyrus, and say unto him, Thus saith the Lord God; Thou sealest up the sum, full of wisdom, and perfect in beauty. Thou hast been in Eden the garden of God; every precious stone was thy covering, the sardius, topaz, and the diamond, the beryl, the onyx, and the jasper, the sapphire, the emerald, and the carbuncle, and gold: the workmanship of thy tabrets and of thy pipes was prepared in thee in the day that thou wast created. Thou art the anointed cherub that covereth: and I have set thee so: thou wast upon the holy mountain of God; thou hast walked up and down in the midst of the stones of fire. Thou wast perfect in thy ways from the day that thou wast created, till iniquity was found in thee.

Ezekiel 28:12-15

1. In the beginning, Satan was created as a perfect

_____.

2. His angelic name was _____.

3. He was created with a _____ will.

4. Because he sinned, he was cast out of Heaven, as were all of the angels who chose to _____ and follow Lucifer's attack on God.

For if God spared not the angels that sinned, but cast them down to hell, and delivered them into chains of darkness, to be reserved unto judgment.

2 Peter 2:4

And there was war in heaven: Michael and his angels fought against the dragon; and the dragon fought and his angels, And prevailed not; neither was their place found any more in heaven. And the great dragon was cast out, that old serpent, called the Devil, and Satan, which deceiveth the whole world: he was cast out into the earth, and his angels were cast out with him. And I heard a loud voice saying in heaven, Now is come salvation, and strength, and the kingdom of our God, and the power of his Christ: for the accuser of our brethren is cast down, which accused them before our God day and night.

Revelation 12:7-10

Christ Unlimited — P.O. Box 850 — Dewey, AZ 86327 USA

And there appeared another wonder in heaven; and behold a great red dragon, having seven heads and ten horns, and seven crowns upon his heads. And his tail drew the third part of the stars of heaven, and did cast them to the earth: and the dragon stood before the woman which was ready to be delivered, for to devour her child as soon as it was born.

Revelation 12:3,4

5. What sin caused Satan to be cast out of Heaven?

_____

How art thou fallen from heaven, O Lucifer, son of the morning! how art thou cut down to the ground, which didst weaken the nations! For thou hast said in thine heart, I will ascend into heaven, I will exalt my throne above the stars of God: I will sit also upon the mount of the congregation, in the sides of the north: I will ascend above the heights of the clouds: I will be like the most High. Yet thou shalt be brought down to hell, to the sides of the pit.

Isaiah 14:12-15

6. Satan set his will against God's will by declaring "I will" how many times in the above verse? _____

7. Man's sin today is the same as Lucifer's, which was:

_____

C. God never meant for evil to exist. He did not create evil,
   only the situation in which it can exist. _____ is simply
   the opposite of _____, and as it takes free will for evil
   to come into existence, Lucifer was the first created being to
   exercise his will against God.

Let no man say when he is tempted, I am tempted of God: for
God cannot be tempted with evil, neither tempteth he any
man: But every man is tempted, when he is drawn away of
his own lust, and enticed. Then when lust hath conceived, it
bringeth forth sin: and sin, when it is finished, bringeth forth
death. Do not err, my beloved brethren. Every good gift and
every perfect gift is from above, and cometh down from the
Father of lights, with whom is no variableness, neither shadow of turning. Of his own will begat he us with the word of
truth, that we should be a kind of firstfruits of his creatures.
                        James 1:13-18

I form the light, and create darkness: I make peace, and
create evil: I the Lord do all these things.
                        Isaiah 45:7

1. Every _____ and _____ gift comes from God.

2. All evil comes from _____ and _____.

3. God did not create evil by <u>making</u> something evil; He only created the situation that would allow evil to exist. That situation was to give His created beings a _____ to do evil or good.

> See, I have set before thee this day life and good, and death and evil... I call heaven and earth to record this day against you, that I have set before you life and death, blessing and cursing: therefore choose life, that both thou and thy seed may live.
>
> Deuteronomy 30:15,19

Also, see Deuteronomy 30:16-20.

4. God has not allowed Satan to exist on this earth without providing the remedy and power to _____ him.

> Submit yourselves therefore to God. Resist the devil, and he will flee from you.
>
> James 4:7

> He that committeth sin is of the devil; for the devil sinneth from the beginning. For this purpose the Son of God was manifested, that he might destroy the works of the devil.
>
> 1 John 3:8

Christ Unlimited — P.O. Box 850 — Dewey, AZ 86327   USA

And the seventy returned again with joy, saying, Lord, even the devils are subject unto us through thy name. And he said unto them, I beheld Satan as lightning fall from heaven. Behold, I give unto you power to tread on serpents and scorpions, and over all the power of the enemy: and nothing shall by any means hurt you. Notwithstanding in this rejoice not, that the spirits are subject unto you; but rather rejoice, because your names are written in heaven.

Luke 10:17-20

Also see Mark 16:17,18; 1 John 4:4.

These things I have spoken unto you, that in me ye might have peace. In the world ye shall have tribulation: but be of good cheer; I have overcome the world.

John 16:33

II. Recognizing Satan's Devices

A. How do we recognize Satan's devices?

_____.

References: 2 Thessalonians 2:8-17; 2 Timothy 3:14-17

B. Should we study books of an occult nature to learn about Satan? _____

And have no fellowship with the unfruitful works of darkness, but rather reprove them. For it is a shame even to speak of those things which are done of them in secret. But all things that are reproved are made manifest by the light: for whatsoever doth make manifest is light.

Ephesians 5:11-13

C. Do new Christians need those who are older and more mature in the Lord to help them discern evil? _____

For every one that useth milk is unskilful in the word of righteousness: for he is a babe. But strong meat belongeth to them that are of full age, even those who by reason of use have their senses exercised to discern both good and evil.

Hebrews 5:13,14

D. Specifically: What are some of Satan's devices, according to the scripture references beneath each statement?

1. Satan wants us to be _____ of him.

Lest Satan should get an advantage of us: for we are not ignorant of his devices.

2 Corinthians 2:11

Christ Unlimited — P.O. Box 850 — Dewey, AZ 86327   USA

Having the understanding darkened, being alienated from the life of God through the ignorance that is in them, because of the blindness of their heart.

>   Ephesians 4:18

2. Satan wants us to _____ him.

Be sober, be vigilant; because your adversary the devil, as a roaring lion, walketh about, seeking whom he may devour.

>   1 Peter 5:8

For God hath not given us the spirit of fear; but of power, and of love, and of a sound mind.

>   2 Timothy 1:7

There is no fear in love; but perfect love casteth out fear: because fear hath torment. He that feareth is not made perfect in love.

>   1 John 4:18

3. Satan wants us to _____ God for our problems.
   Reference: Genesis 3:1-5

(Everyone wants to blame someone else for his, or her, problems. Adam blamed Eve (Gen. 3:12), and Eve blamed the serpent. Job blamed God (Job 30:19-21). The truth, however, is far different.)

Christ Unlimited — P.O. Box 850 — Dewey, AZ 86327   USA

The righteous cry, and the Lord heareth, and delivereth them out of all their troubles.

Psalm 34:17

Therefore hearken unto me, ye men of understanding: far be it from God, that he should do wickedness; and from the Almighty, that he should commit iniquity. For the work of a man shall he render unto him, and cause every man to find according to his ways. Yea, surely God will not do wickedly, neither will the Almighty pervert judgment.

Job 34:10-12

4. Satan tries to convince Christians that they have no _____ over him, but rather that he has _____ over them.

To open their eyes, and to turn them from darkness to light, and from the power of Satan unto God, that they may receive forgiveness of sins, and inheritance among them which are sanctified by faith that is in me.

Acts 26:18

Behold, I give unto you power to tread on serpents and scorpions, and over all the power of the enemy: and nothing shall by any means hurt you.

Luke 10:19

Christ Unlimited — P.O. Box 850 — Dewey, AZ 86327   USA

5. Satan does not want us to know that the only power he has over any Christian is the power of _____.

And the great dragon was cast out, that old serpent, called the Devil, and Satan, which deceiveth the whole world: he was cast out into the earth, and his angels were cast out with him. And I heard a loud voice saying in heaven, Now is come salvation, and strength, and the kingdom of our God, and the power of his Christ: for the accuser of our brethren is cast down, which accused them before our God day and night. And they overcame him by the blood of the Lamb, and by the word of their testimony; and they loved not their lives unto the death.

Revelation 12:9-11

But be ye doers of the word, and not hearers only, deceiving your own selves.

James 1:22

For they that are such serve not our Lord Jesus Christ, but their own belly; and by good words and fair speeches deceive the hearts of the simple.

Romans 16:18

Christ Unlimited — P.O. Box 850 — Dewey, AZ 86327   USA

Overcoming Life Memory Verse

The suggested memory verse for this lesson is:

And they overcame him (the devil) by the blood of the Lamb, and by the word of their testimony; and they loved not their lives unto the death.

Revelation 12:11

Review Outline, Section One

[Author's Note: See Chapter 1, pp. 1-15, in <u>Exposing Satan's Devices</u>.]

I. Satan's Identity

A. Former heavenly cherub, or angelic being

1. Called Lucifer **(Isaiah 14:12-15)**

2. Gifted with beauty

3. Gifted with intelligence

4. Covered the Throne of God with beauty and music

5. Walked on the Holy mountain of God

(Isaiah 14:12-15; Ezekiel 28:12-19)

B. Lucifer, now Satan:

1. Is a fallen angelic being

2. Is now roaming the earth and Hades

II. Satan's Fall

A. Satan's Rebellion **(Ezekiel 28:12-19)**

1. He was the first to exercise free will against God.

2. Satan's sins were:

a. Pride — He thought he was equal to God.

b. Rebellion — He wanted to usurp God's power.

c. Self-will — He resisted God's will, which is sin.

3. He waged war on God **(Revelation 12:7-12)**.

a. One-third of the angels joined him (Revelation 12:4).

b. An archangel named <u>Michael</u> led God's warriors against him. (Revelation 12:7; Jude 9).

c. Satan and his angels were defeated in Heaven.

B. Satan's Punishment

(Matthew 25:41; Revelation 20:10-15)

1. Cast down to earth

2. Given a limited time (set by God) to do evil

3. Is to experience final defeat and eternity in the lake of fire

4. Has no remaining status with God

C. Satan's Power

1. Over spirits and men:

a. Evil spirits (demons and fallen angels)

b. Dead unbelievers

c. Unsaved human beings

1) Beginning with Adam and Eve's day (Genesis 3:7-14)

2) Continues today (Romans 1:18-32)

d. Back-slidden Christians, who are:

1) Deceived Christians, who have moved out of the will of God

2) Rebellious Christians, who are disobedient

3) Passive Christians, who lack a regular and consistent prayer life

Christ Unlimited — P.O. Box 850 — Dewey, AZ 86327   USA

4) Ignorant Christians, who lack knowledge of the Bible

2. Purpose of Satan's Devices:

   a. To distract Christians:

      1) From reading the Word

      2) From praying

      3) From fellowshipping with other believers

   b. To get back at God:

      1) By defiling God's children

      2) By turning God's own children against Him

Review Outline Quiz, Section One

1. Who was thrown out of Heaven?

   _____

2. What is the final destination of Satan and his followers?

   _____

3. List three scriptures that show Christians have power over
   Satan and demons.

   _____

4. Put these events in Satan's past and future in order:
   (Answer on each line will be a, b, c, d, e, or f.)

   a. Thrown out of Heaven.   _____
   b. Thrown into the lake of fire.   _____
   c. Rebelled against God.   _____
   d. Called Lucifer.   _____
   e. Fought the Archangel Michael   _____
   f. Roamed the earth.   _____

5. All sin, evil, and bad things come from Satan:
   True _____ or False _____

6. What were Satan's sins?

   _____, _____, _____

7. What four types of beings does Satan have power over?

   a. _____

   b. _____

   c. _____

   d. _____

8. Name three purposes of Satan's devices:

   a. _____

   b. _____

   c. _____

9. What is the only way Satan can have power over believers?

   _____

10. What is the ultimate way we can defeat Satan?

   _____

Exposing Satan's Devices Workbook

Section Two

"Satanic Deception — His Evil Tactic"

Christ Unlimited — P.O. Box 850 — Dewey, AZ 86327   USA

Exposing Satan's Devices Workbook
Section Two: "Satanic Deception — His Evil Tactic"
Expository Introduction

The Bible tells us that all of mankind has followed Satan because of one reason — that reason being <u>deception</u>. We have all been deceived by the devil at different times. Before we began to follow Christ, we were not even aware of the enemy's tactics. Revelation 12:9-11 says:

And the great dragon was cast out, that old serpent, called the Devil, and Satan, which <u>deceiveth the whole world</u>: he was cast out into the earth, and his angels were cast out with him. And I heard a loud voice saying in heaven, Now is come salvation, and strength, and the kingdom of our God, and the power of his Christ: for the accuser of our brethren is cast down, which accused them before our God day and night. And they overcame him by the blood of the Lamb, and the word of their testimony; and they loved not their lives unto the death.

Revelation 12:11 tells us that we overcome the devil by the blood of Jesus. What Jesus did by His death, burial, and resurrection was to obtain the victory over the devil for all who give their lives to Him unto the death. Praise God! Through Jesus we can overcome the devil's lies and his deception. In fact, the only weapon Satan has against us is the power to deceive us. However, if we have the truth, he can no longer deceive us, and we can walk in victory.

In this lesson, we are going to see what deception causes men to do and what some of the methods and tactics are that the devil uses against Christians. Let's look first at some of the reasons why men are following Satan's deceptions.

One of the first reasons is that men are ignorant of God's Word. Hosea 4:6 says, My people are destroyed for lack of knowledge. Even after we know God, the devil can take advantage of us unless we study the Word of God so we can understand the devil's devices.

Second Corinthians 2:11 says, Lest Satan should get an advantage of us: for we are not ignorant of his devices.

Another reason some men follow the devil is because they have deliberately chosen to do so. Romans 1:29-32 speaks of these people.

Being filled with all unrighteousness, fornication, wickedness, covetousness, maliciousness: full of envy, murder, debate, deceit, malignity; whisperers, backbiters, haters of God, despiteful, proud, boasters, inventors of evil things, disobedient to parents, without understanding, covenant breakers, without natural affection, implacable, unmerciful: Who knowing the judgment of God, that they which commit such things are worthy of death, not only do the same, but have pleasure in them that do them.

Christ Unlimited — P.O. Box 850 — Dewey, AZ 86327   USA

Those who knowingly follow Satan are damned, because they have utterly rejected the price Jesus paid on the cross as the penalty for their sins. Therefore, they will be damned for rejecting Jesus, not for their sins (Mark 16:16).

However, the majority of people who follow Satan's ways fit the pattern the Apostle Paul described in Ephesians 4:18,19, who:

...Having the understanding darkened, being alienated from the life of God through the ignorance that is in them, because of the blindness of their heart: Who being past feeling have given themselves over unto lasciviousness, to work all uncleanness with greediness.

They simply do not recognize Satan and his various devices. Not only do they not have righteousness in their lives — they do not want it! When anyone decides to follow his own way, that is self-will and selfishness, and those characteristics are part of Satan's nature. So, when we seek our own ways out of the flesh or carnal natures, we are following the devil whether we know it, or whether we intend to or not.

The secular "religion" of humanism today says, "Do your own thing, no matter what anyone else says. You have your rights!"

Those who follow that philosophy are serving the devil and his purposes. They are like those who live in the last days Paul wrote to Timothy about:

This know also, that in the last days perilous times shall come. For men shall be lovers of their own selves, covetous, boasters, proud, blasphemers, disobedient to parents, unthankful, unholy, without natural affection, trucebreakers, false accusers, incontinent, fierce, despisers of those that are good, traitors, heady, highminded, lovers of pleasures more than lovers of God.

2 Timothy 3:1-4

Every person who has ever lived is going to face a crossroads at some time in his life, a place where a decision must be made to receive or reject Jesus. Even children face this decision at a certain age. This time in a child's life comes when he or she reaches the "age of accountability." That is when they realize there is a God, and they are responsible to make decisions to seek Him or reject him.

Romans 1:19, 20 makes it clear that men are without excuse, because even creation itself testifies there is a God.

Because that which may be known of God is manifest in them; for God hath shewed it unto them. For the invisible things of him from the creation of the world are clearly seen, being understood by the things that are made, even his eternal power and Godhead; so that they are without excuse.

Babies and children who die under the age of accountability will not go to hell, as they remain under God's grace and love and will go to Heaven.

Christ Unlimited — P.O. Box 850 — Dewey, AZ 86327   USA

There is no excuse for people in the United States to go to Hell. We have had the gospel preached freely from the time this country was discovered until now. In spite of the increasing media and governmental harrassment, the gospel is still going forth over the air waves and in churches. Our mission as the Church is to take the gospel to the rest of the world who have not had the opportunity to hear the good news. Why should we evangelize our people over and over while many in the world have never once heard of the name of Jesus?

How Satan Deceives Mankind

Satan's methods for deceiving men include the following:

(1) He tries to get us to challenge God's laws and instructions, as Eve did (Gen. 3).

(2) He causes us to sin through disobedience, at which point, we immediately act as Adam and Eve did: We hide from God out of fear. (Christians who sin tend to stop coming to church, instead of running into the next service and falling at the altar to repent and receive forgiveness.)

(3) He causes us to doubt God's goodness, mercy, and love. Thoughts such as this are dropped into our minds: "If God really cares for me, why hasn't He answered my prayers yet?" If our prayers are not answered yet, and they are prayed according to God's will, then it is because of something in our lives that is blocking our answers, or because somehow the devil is hindering our answers from coming.

We need to learn to defend the Father, when the devil comes in with those doubts and negative thoughts. The Father's heart toward us is the same as a good earthly father's heart is toward his children. He loves, cares for, protects, and nurtures his children, never doing evil toward them. He only wants good things for them (Matt. 7:11).

(4) Another method Satan uses to deceive men is that he tempts us to act independently of God. We have been given access to the wisest and best counsel in Heaven and earth through prayer and God's Word; and yet many times, we do not seek His counsel. Instead, we just do what <u>we</u> think is best.

God will not interfere in our lives if we do not want him to. He will not override the right to choose since he has given that right to all mankind.

(5) Satan also deceives us by tempting us to commit carnal sins in three main ways (1 John 2:16):

    a. <u>Lust of the flesh</u>

    b. <u>Lust of the eyes</u>

    c. <u>Pride of life</u>

These three things combined are called "the love of the world." They cover all of the sins of the soul (mind, will, and emotions) and body. Eve saw that the fruit of the forbidden tree was to be desired. Through the lust of her eyes, her flesh began to lust after the fruit. Then she allowed herself to believe that God had deceived them,

Christ Unlimited — P.O. Box 850 — Dewey, AZ 86327   USA

that the fruit really was for their benefit and would not mean their destruction.

From then on, Satan has used those three things to permeate human society with the desire for the following things: worldly riches, advantages in life, status and position, pleasures of the body, intellectual pursuits, science (that thinks there is no God, and it is the final authority), medicine, business, religious systems, arts and other cultural pursuits that the soul lusts after, and political systems that have men vying for power and control. These pursuits apart from God become snares.

Satan rules over the world systems, because Adam lost his dominion when he and Eve sinned. However, Jesus took the authority and dominion back from Satan on the cross and delegated it to His Church, which has not lived up to her assignment as yet. That does not mean the Church is to rule the world through secular institutions or religious establishments.

God's kingdom is the only kingdom in which we are to rule. This rule is done in the Spirit through God's love and power. For Jesus and His Body to have dominion means we are to transform society around us by our spiritual examples (be "the light and salt of the world") and take the gospel to the ends of the earth.

By changing men's hearts, the world around us is changed. Men in the world try to change the outward systems and laws, but that never produces the changes they desire, as those changes can only come through an inward transformation. When Jesus comes back, all of the present world systems will be swept away, and God's systems and principles for society to live by will be set up.

We have to live in the midst of the things of the world, but we must not love them and embrace them as part of the Christian walk. Anything in the world (such as the money system) that we have to be involved in should be committed to Jesus and handled according to His purposes and principles. Otherwise it becomes evil to us.

(6) The next method Satan uses to deceive mankind is to encourage men to go the way of self. The degree to which we worship or serve self reflects the degree to which we are yielding to the ways of Satan. He is the very essence of self-seeking. We need to do what God wants us to do each day in His service, or we are serving self.

> The Lord knoweth how to deliver the godly out of temptations, and to reserve the unjust unto the day of judgment to be punished: But chiefly them that walk after the flesh in the lust of uncleanness, and despise government. Presumptuous are they, selfwilled, they are not afraid to speak evil of dignities.
>
> 2 Peter 2:9,10

God says that selfishness is a form of rebellion; therefore, the selfish do not respect authority.

(7) Satan also tries to deceive men into believing they are doing the will of God when they really are in areas that are sinful (2 Cor.

11:14). We can be deceived by the devil appearing as "an angel of light" (which really is an angel of darkness), if we do not walk carefully and humbly with God daily. We can have spiritual pride which opens the door for the devil to deceive us in the spiritual realm.

(8) Another way in which the devil masquerades as an "angel of light" is called "a wolf in sheep's clothing." That means men who come into a church or area, not as true ministers, but simply to plunder, steal from, and destroy the flock of God (Matt. 7:15,16). These men may appear at first to be preaching the truth, so we must "prove" and "test" what they say and be sensitive to a witness from the Holy Spirit. Even if they say the right things, we are to judge their fruits, not just their words. Men who fall under the spell of an angel of light or a spirit of greed usually are those who begin cults and false religions.

We can know God's true people by the fruit of their lives (Gal. 5:22,23), not necessarily by how much they seem to minister in the gifts of the Spirit. Satan has counterfeits of those supernatural manifestations. He also is a supernatural being and lives in that realm. People who fall for the lies of false prophets are those who do not know the Word of God very well for themselves.

Satan has no new lies — just new victims.

(9) Another deceptive method Satan uses is that he tries to encourage pride in men. That was his first characteristic of iniquity, so he wants to corrupt as many of those created in the image of

God as he can. <u>The root of all sin is pride</u>. Satan is jealous of God's people, because he was <u>not</u> created in the image of God. Although he was created with a free will, he found no redemption as did man.

The reason for this, is that when Lucifer sinned, he committed the unpardonable sin — he sinned with full knowledge and revelation of what he was doing against God. Adam and Eve did not have this knowledge of good and evil prior to their temptation, so they sinned in innocence; therefore, there was a way of redemption made back to God through Jesus Christ's atonement.

Satan's pride was his downfall, and he tries to get men to commit this same evil. There are two definitions of pride: 1) a too-high opinion of oneself (or haughtiness, arrogance, and egotism) and 2) a sense of dignity, self-respect, and self-esteem as being of value to God because Jesus died for us. God wants us to feel good about ourselves, but not to think more highly of ourselves than we ought.

> For I say, through the grace given unto me, to every man that is among you, not to think of himself more highly than he ought to think; but to think soberly, according as God hath dealt to every man the measure of faith.
>
> Romans 12:3

Pride in the sense of Satan's characteristic leads to unbelief. It is a deadly trap, especially "spiritual pride," which is very subtle some-

Christ Unlimited — P.O. Box 850 — Dewey, AZ 86327   USA

times. It shows up as arrogance in regard to the gifts, knowledge, and abilities that God has given us.

We need to minister to others in love, in order to win people to the Lord, to cause them to want what we have. Ministering out of a "know-it-all" attitude is not love. In **1 Corinthians 8:1**, Paul wrote that **knowledge puffeth up, but love edifies.** So when we begin to gain knowledge from God's Word and from the Holy Spirit, we need to make sure that our love for God and others also is increasing.

Christians ought never to boast in themselves over things God has provided for us or entrusted to us. The <u>glory</u> belongs to the Almighty. **Proverbs 16:18** tells what happens to those who embrace pride:

> Pride goeth before destruction, and an haughty spirit before a fall.

(10) Another method Satan uses is attempting to cause us to act hastily or rashly, while the Holy Spirit is gentle and patient, not pushy or rude. If the devil gets us to make a decision in haste or under pressure, more than likely, we will pay for it later. Many a Christian has married in haste, or gotten involved in a business partnership, to his or her later regret.

Any kind of partnership should be prayed over earnestly until it becomes a certainty that it is God's will. For the same reason, decisions should not be made with haste. However, when we do make commitments, we should keep them. We can tell that something is not right about what we are planning or considering if we are in a lot of confusion or have anxiety and restlessness. Isaiah 57:19-21 tells us that God always brings us rest and peace. James 3:17 also tells us that the wisdom from above is peaceful.

(11) Another tactic of the enemy is to cause men to follow false religions. Since Satan is a counterfeiter, he wants to spread a counterfeit gospel and set up false gods (demons) around the world for people to worship. In Exodus 20:3-6, God made it plain that His people are to have no other gods before Him. A "god" is anything that a person places in a position of more importance in life than God Himself.

One deceptive "god" is thinking that we can <u>earn</u> salvation by works. Our works can become gods, because our trust is in them, not in the Lord God Almighty; whose salvation is a free gift. There can be many things in life that are gods to people. The god of Humanism is worship of mankind, or <u>self</u>.

<u>When we worship anything except God, we are worshiping an idol</u>.

An idol can be an object made out of any kind of material, a "mythical" or demonic (false religion) character, a mental idea, or material things. Some men "worship" addictive substances. Other people "worship" food or sex. Some "worship" money, possessions, or power.

False religions never include:

— The basic doctrines of the Church, such as the virgin birth

— A belief in a literal Heaven and Hell (Mark 9:43,44)

— That Jesus was all man <u>and</u> all divine — the only <u>way</u> to be saved from eternal damnation. They will usually teach that He was only a man, although a "good" man (John 14:6)

— The fact that His blood paid the price for all sin, past, present, and future, and that through His blood is the only way anyone can have his sins atoned for and see God (1 John 1:7)

— The fact that He is coming back for His people (Acts 1:11)

A cult is any form of religious worship or sect that differs from basic Bible doctrines, or that says there is another way to be saved than Christ. Cults sometimes have threads of truth from the Bible, but are in gross error in other areas of Bible doctrine.

Even some churches that are otherwise sound in doctrine have slipped into "cultic practices" because they add to or take away from the Word of God. We should feel great sympathy for those caught in these traps of Satan, because they represent the earnest attempts of millions of people to find fulfillment of the deep legitimate needs of the human spirit.

Anyone who has been involved with any false religion or cult should renounce it and seek God in order for truth to replace error in the mind and heart.

In this lesson, we have looked at some of the major methods and tactics that Satan uses to deceive us. Being aware of these can help us avoid them and combat attacks of the enemy.

Lesson for Section Two

[Author's Note: Chapter 1 and pages 17-20 of Chapter 2 of <u>Exposing Satan's Devices</u> are covered in this lesson, also the material in the expository introduction. Please read this material before beginning the lesson.]

I. Satan Deceives Men

Satan's deception leads men astray. Men choose deception because:

A. They are _____.

Reference: Ephesians 4:18

B. They deliberately _____ to follow the devil.
Reference: Romans 1:29-32

C. They choose to follow their _____, thus they are following the devil. Selfishness is part of his nature.
Reference: 2 Timothy 3:2

D. Other people utterly _____ Jesus, and therefore, they are also followers of Satan.
Reference: Mark 16:16

II. Satan's Deceptive Methods

Some of Satan's methods for deceiving men are:

A. To cause them to challenge God's _____ to man
Reference: Genesis 3:1-6

B. To cause men to _____ God's goodness and provision

Reference: Matthew 14:31

C. To _____ man to act through his own lust

Reference: James 1:13-15

D. To encourage men to go the way of _____

[Satan epitomizes self-seeking.]

Reference: 2 Peter 2:9,10

E. To deceive men into thinking they are doing the _____

_____, when they are in sin or disobedience

Reference: Ephesians 5:6,17

F. To encourage _____ in men

Reference: 1 Timothy 3:6

   1. Define the two kinds of pride.

      a. _____

      b. _____

   2. Satan's unusual _____ was one of the causes of his downfall. It contributed to the development of pride.

Thine heart was lifted up because of thy <u>beauty</u>, thou hast corrupted thy wisdom by reason of thy brightness: I will cast thee to the ground, I will lay thee before kings, that they may behold thee.

Ezekiel 28:17

3. People in today's world are seeking beauty as never before. Beauty aids, make-up, glamorous clothes, beautiful homes, and plush automobiles are only a few of the things the world seeks today. In themselves, these things are not evil, but the _____ for them is ungodly.
   Reference: 1 John 2:15-17

4. Spiritual pride also is a deadly trap. What is it?

   _____

   _____

   Reference: 1 Corinthians 1:29-31, 8:1b

5. What happens to someone who embraces pride?

   _____

   Reference: Proverbs 16:18

G. Satan also tries to tempt men to sin carnally. The three main temptations Satan uses are:

   1. _____

   2. _____

   3. _____

   Reference: 1 John 2:16

4. Those three things together make up the _____ of the _____. Satan has dominion over human society with its riches, advantages, pleasures, intellectual pursuits,

etc. This does not mean we cannot have things. It means we are not to lust after them, or put them ahead of God.

H. Satan also tries to come through men as _____ in sheep's clothing, to plunder, to steal from, and to destroy the flock of God.

References: Matthew 7:15,16; John 10:10

1. Satan has no new lies, just new _____. His victims are those who believe him.

2. God has made a way for us to _____ every temptation.

Reference: 1 Corinthians 10:13

I. Satan also tries to cause us to act _____.

1. The Holy Spirit is _____, not pushy or rude.

2. Anxiety and restlessness are from _____.

3. God's will brings _____ and _____.

References: Proverbs 14:29, 21:5, 29:20; James 3:17

But the wicked are like the troubled sea, when it cannot rest, whose waters cast up mire and dirt. There is no peace, saith my God, to the wicked.

Isaiah 57:20,21

J. Another method of Satan is to try to cause men to follow false _____ and _____.

(Satan is a counterfeiter, and he wants to set up false gods and spread counterfeit religions.)

Reference: **Exodus 20:3-6**

1. Define what a "god" is:

   _____

   _____

2. When a person worships anything or anyone other than the God of the Bible, we say that person is worshiping an

   _____.

3. An idol may be:

   a. _____

   b. _____

   c. _____

4. Some people worship:

   a. _____

   b. _____

   c. _____

   d. _____

   e. _____

   f. _____

   g. _____

5. The Christian definition of God is:

_____

III. False Religions

False religions do not teach the true Gospel or Christian doctrine, which includes the following foundational truths.

A. _____

But if we walk in the light, as he is in the light, we have fellowship one with another, and the blood of Jesus Christ his Son cleanseth us from all sin.

1 John 1:7

B. _____

Which also said, Ye men of Galilee, why stand ye gazing up into heaven? this same Jesus, which is taken up from you into heaven, shall so come in like manner as ye have seen him go into heaven.

Acts 1:11

C. _____

And if thy hand offend thee, cut it off: it is better for thee to enter into life maimed, than having two hands to go into hell, into the fire that never shall be quenched.

Mark 9:43,44

Christ Unlimited — P.O. Box 850 — Dewey, AZ 86327   USA

D. _____

> Jesus saith unto him, I am the way, the truth, and the life: no man cometh unto the Father, but by me.
>
> John 14:6

IV. Cultic Religions

(Satan promotes false doctrines and religions through "cults.")

A. What is a cult?

1. According to a dictionary: _____

_____

2. According to Christian teaching: _____

_____

B. Cults sometimes have _____ of truth from the Bible, but are in gross error in one or more of the Bible doctrines.

C. Some churches have entered into cultic practices, because they have embraced doctrines that either "add to" or "take away from" the _____.

> For I testify unto every man that heareth the words of the prophecy of this book, If any man shall add unto these things, God shall add unto him the plagues that are written in this book.
>
> Revelation 22:18

Christ Unlimited — P.O. Box 850 — Dewey, AZ 86327   USA

And if any man shall take away from the words of the book of this prophecy, God shall take away his part out of the book of life, and out of the holy city, and from the things which are written in this book.

Revelation 22:19

D. Some cults have a greater percentage of error than others, but any degree of _____ leads to God's disapproval.

What thing soever I command you, observe to do it: thou shalt not add thereto, nor diminish from it.

Deuteronomy 12:32

(Please read pages 18 and 19 of Exposing Satan's Devices for a list of major cults and false religious movements.)

E. These cults represent millions of people seeking _____ _____.
Many of these people seem not to have found fulfillment of their spiritual needs in some established churches. This is why we need the power of the Holy Spirit in our churches.

F. Some people have found _____ in spite of doctrinal errors of the cults. The Holy Spirit always attempts to lead people out from under the bondage of false sects.

G. The way of the masses is not the _____ Jesus spoke of.

Enter ye in at the strait gate: for wide is the gate, and broad is the way, that leadeth to destruction, and many there be which go in thereat: Because strait is the gate, and narrow is the way, which leadeth unto life, and few there be that find it.

Matthew 7:13,14

H. True religion is not a particular church or denomination, but a _____ with Jesus Christ and an attitude of the heart. The Kingdom of God is within.

And when he was demanded of the Pharisees, when the kingdom of God should come, he answered them and said, The kingdom of God cometh not with observation: Neither shall they say, Lo here! or, lo there! for, behold, the kingdom of God is within you.

Luke 17:20,21

I. A person who has been involved with false religions or cults should _____.

Overcoming Life Memory Verse

The suggested memory verse for this lesson is:

The thief cometh not, but for to steal, and to kill, and to destroy: I am come that they might have life, and that they might have it more abundantly.

John 10:10

Review Outline, Section Two

[Author's Note: This outline covers pp. 17-20, <u>Exposing Satan's</u> <u>Devices</u>.]

I. Satan's Devices

   A. To deceive Christians:

      1. By appearing as a false angel of light, counterfeiting the Holy Spirit (2 Corinthians 11:13-15)

      2. To cause impatience with the speed at which God moves (1 Samuel 13:8-14)

   B. To rob, steal, kill, and destroy (John 10:10)

   C. To tempt and bring anxiety (Psalm 95:8-11; 1 Corinthians 10:13)

   D. To bring deception and lies (John 8:44) to confuse believers and alienate them from God and one another

   E. To ensnare men into false beliefs

II. False Religions and Cults

   A. False religions (counterfeit Christianity) can be detected:

      1. If beliefs deviate from basic doctrines (Hebrews 6:1,2)

      2. If they do not teach the atoning blood of Jesus

      3. If they do not believe in Jesus' literal second coming

      4. If they do not believe in a literal Heaven and Hell

      5. If they teach more than one Way to eternal life with God

B. False religion leads to idolatry, which is:

  1. Putting anything or anyone ahead of God

  2. Worshipping anything but God (**Exodus 20:3-5**)

  3. Making anything but God the center of life (**Colossians 3:5**)

Review Outline Quiz, Section Two

1. What does the "thief" come to do (John 10:10)?

   _____

2. List three devices that Satan uses.

   To _____, _____, and _____

3. What is an "angel of light" (2 Corinthians 11:13-15)?

   _____

4. What do false religions lead to? _____

5. What is idolatry? _____

   _____

   _____

6. List three things that distinguish false religions.

   a. _____

   b. _____

   c. _____

7. Satan's deception and lies can do three things?

   _____, _____, or _____ believers.

8. Who is responsible for testing and proving doctrines? _____

9. What are doctrines "tested and proved" by? _____

10. All false religions or cults are_____of Christianity.

Exposing Satan's Devices Workbook

Section Three

"Walking on Enemy Territory"

Christ Unlimited — P.O. Box 850 — Dewey, AZ 86327   USA

Exposing Satan's Devices Workbook
Section Three: "Walking on Enemy Territory"
Expository Introduction

This is the third of six lessons examining the methods and devices Satan uses to deceive people and keep them from coming to know Jesus Christ. We should be knowledgeable concerning the devil's tactics in order to better resist him. The last lesson ended with a look at "cults" and false religions. This lesson will concentrate on the <u>occult</u>.

The word <u>occult</u> actually means "hidden, secret, or unseen." The devil uses the movement of occultism to involve people in hidden works of darkness. He is the master ruler of darkness, who entices people into his hidden realm.

Many cults may appear to be Christian, Godly, or good to some degree, but many occult and satanic groups make no such claims. They are not camouflaged with any threads of Christianity, but openly operate in the dark secrets of the devil and demonism. Some New Age groups, although occult in nature, do operate in deception by clothing themselves in some aspects of Christianity. However, these groups will not profess to believe in the basic tenets of the Bible, such as the divinity of Jesus. Instead, He is called "an advanced Master," or some such title.

Cults usually concentrate on teachings and doctrines, sets of beliefs that vary from the mainstream Church or society in some way. However, occult groups offer their participants evil supernatural power. Satan's demons operate in counterfeit gifts of the Holy Spirit, such as false healing, false speaking in tongues, and false prophecy.

The Christian battle against the ruler of darkness, however, is a spiritual battle that must be waged against supernatural beings, not against other people.

There has never been a time in history when the warnings against occultism were more necessary than at present. Eastern religions are growing at an alarming rate in the United States, and while they are false religions, at the same time, they incorporate a great degree of occultism. Diciplines such as yoga and the martial arts are rooted in Eastern mysticism (occult practices) that is the foundation of the Eastern religions.

Millions of non-Christians as well as many Christians suffer physical, mental, emotional, and spiritual oppression, but few ever realizc that those things are happening because they became ensnared in the web of occultism. Any involvement with the occult means the participant has walked into the enemy's territory and come under at least a certain amount of his control.

Occultism involves:

Astrology, spiritism or necromancy (holding supposed conversations with the dead through a human "medium"), sorcery and magic, divination, fortune telling, "water witching" or dowsing (using a stick to find water), and even tattooing.

Little Things Can Be Dangerous

Leviticus 19:28 says it is forbidden "to mark the skin," and that is because "tattooing" with paint, needles, or knife pricks already was a witchcraft practice of false religions. If a Christian already has a tattoo, he should ask the Lord to remove any curse attached to it.

It may seem like a little thing but Solomon wrote:

Take us the foxes, the little foxes, that spoil the vines: for our vines have tender grapes.

Song of Solomon 2:15

Foxes sometimes, in search of food, would enter into the grape orchards, devour the grapes, and spoil the crop. However, the little foxes were too small to reach the grape bunches, so they would chew on the vines, and that would kill the whole vine. Instead of the farmer just losing his crop, he would lose his vine, which was more disastrous. Spiritually, some things we do, or allow, that we might think are little or insignificant also can be disastrous for us.

One of these "little foxes" we see today is parents allowing their children to mark or tattoo their bodies. Any Christian can look at someone who has tattoos all over them and be repulsed by it and know by discernment that it is not God. However, the same Christians may get a small tattoo themselves or allow their children to have one without thinking anything about it.

Toymakers today even sell washable ink transfer kits so children can mark their bodies with designs. This may seem like a harmless game, but this is the enemy preparing our children early to receive real tattoos later on.

The Bible warns us against tattoos in Leviticus 19:28:

> Ye shall not make any cuttings in your flesh for the dead, nor print any marks upon you: I am the Lord.

Other scriptures, such as 1 Kings 18:28 and Deuteronomy 14:1, also warn us not to disfigure our bodies. When Moses wrote that commandment in Leviticus from the Lord, he was referring to a witchcraft ritual that was done in those lands and times to mourn or memorialize the dead. So tattooing has its origin in witchcraft practices. That is what makes it spiritually dangerous.

People do not realize that having a mark can open the door for satanic attack. It can allow the enemy entrance in their lives. Today, this practice is growing because of Eastern religions and heathen influences that have been infiltrating our nation and which promote tattooing or printing marks on the skin.

Years ago, young boys in the military who were assigned to duty in heathen lands might run across a tattoo parlor and return home with tattoos on their arms or chests. Now these parlors are everywhere in the United States, because our nation has opened its doors to pagan religions.

One of the latest discoveries of how AIDS is transmitted is through dirty drug and tattoo needles. If anyone, through ignorance, has received a tattoo, or has allowed a child or children to have one, that person needs to repent. Then the person should pray against and rebuke any evil that might have entered the house through that "door."

Some tattoos obviously are satanic, as they look devilish, while others may be flowers or other innocent looking designs. But it is the spirit behind this "little fox" that makes it dangerous for a Christian.

Hosea 4:6 says: **My people are destroyed for lack of knowledge.**

Overcomers will put away any things in their lives that amount to "little foxes."

Involvement in the occult is outright disobedience to God's Word and brings a curse upon those who pursue it. (Read **Leviticus 20:27** and **Deuteronomy 7:25,26, 28:14,15.**) Many times a Christian is not able to experience healing in a certain area until past involvement with an occult practice of some kind is repented of and renounced.

This will bring a curse into a Christian's life quicker than any other sin, because it is an open door for Satan to neutralize a Christian's witness and effectiveness for God (Isa. 8:19,20, 47:12-14; Deuteronomy 7:25; and Acts 19:18-20).

Other examples of occultism in today's society include:

Mind control courses, transcendental meditation, acupuncture and acupressure, charms, science of the mind, reincarnation and karma teachings, reading auras, and flying saucers.

Identifying Signs of Cultic and Occultic Groups

Both cults and occult groups tend to have identifying characteristics:

A. They deny that the Lord Jesus Christ is Savior of the world (2 Peter 2:1-3).

B. Their definition of Jesus is not the same as the Christian's understanding. We know that Jesus is truly divine, as well as truly human. But some of these groups declare Jesus to be only human, denying the fact that He is God's only begotten Son (John 3:16). Others consider Him only divine.

C. Cultic organizations deny the virgin birth of Jesus, as do some "Christian" groups, particularly the humanistic denominations and scholars. These mainline churches are usually the same ones who deny that the Bible is the Word of God, but say it is simply legends, stories, and writings of various men down through the centuries.

D. Most deny that His blood is necessary for our atonement. They pride themselves on being a "bloodless" religion. Some go so far as to accuse Christianity of being a barbaric, "bloody" religion, on a par with "ancient religions that offered animal sacrifices."

E. They do not believe that Jesus was resurrected from the dead and will return to earth bodily at the Second Coming. They think He is dead, like Buddha, Muhammed, and other founders of religions.

F. They tend to transform God into a "Great Force," primal thought of the universe, or "the Great Spirit" as many Native Americans do — if they believe at all in a god. Their names for the Godhead include terms such as "the ideal truth or the divine idea," "the greatest personage," "the chief agent of life," and "the glorious spirit creature." Others consider the unity of all mankind as "God."

G. Cults tend to be "clannish" and look on others as lost unless they belong to a particular group. They demand obedience, rather than teach submission to Godly authority.

Submission is taught in God's Word and is the right thing for Christians to do, but it is to be done by choice, not by fear of someone who threatens or coerces them. On the other hand, cultic groups promote "love and acceptance" for everyone, no matter his religion, which means that if someone says Jesus is the only path to God, they simply smile patronizingly and consider that person not as "advanced spiritually" as they are.

H. Reincarnation, the devil's counterfeit of being "born again" is a very big doctrine in occult groups. It is a variation on the old theme of being saved by one's own works, another form of legalism.

This false doctrine teaches that the sum total of one's deeds in this life, good or bad, becomes the "karma" on which the next life depends. If a person behaved more badly than good — cheated people, lied to people and took advantage of them, hurt loved ones, and so forth — then that person would be reborn into a body and/or family where he would be worse off than in the previous life. If a person has been good, his next life may be really great.

Eastern religions, such as Hinduism, take this a step farther into a doctrine called <u>transmigration of souls</u>. That means that bad people may be born again as animals, or even insects! So in India, people cannot kill cows: They might be killing their grandfathers!

I. Another sign of a cult is that leadership tends to heap treasures upon themselves and are self-centered. False shepherds enslave their followers, and this does not mean only in finances. There usually is psychological and spiritual enslavement as well. Slavish devotion to leadership is a requirement for membership.

J. Other signs include the promise of "secret revelation" to group members, the promotion and demand of legalism (**Matt. 23:23**), and not using the same principles and guidelines for the whole person. They may separate spirit, soul, and body as "good" and "bad" parts. (The spirit is called "good" and the body "bad", for example.)

Either the body is totally denied natural desires and needs, or anything is allowed because the body will die and is not a part of the spiritual person. We <u>do</u> need to have our bodies "crucified" with Christ, so that we can walk in sanctification. That means no lusts, no excesses, and no undue emphasis on the body. However, that does not mean that we starve ourselves, (but we should fast as God leads). Neither should we whip ourselves, as some teach as penance for "failing God."

Christ Unlimited — P.O. Box 850 — Dewey, AZ 86327   USA

The body was created by God as a good thing, a "vehicle" in which man could walk around and live on this earth. It is a blessing from the Creator, and is to be His temple while we are on earth, because He lives in us. We need to eat right, exercise, and get enough rest to take care of the temples in which we, and the Holy Spirit, live.

Many False Movements Do Not Believe in Hell

Many false movements teach that hell is nonexistent, a mythological place, or they teach that people who do not agree with their teachings are going there. Also, there is a doctrine called "universalism," or "ultimate reconciliation," which came out of some deceived Christian groups. That teaching is that eventually even Satan and all of the damned will be redeemed. The reasoning is that God is "too good" to condemn any being to eternal torment. They do not understand that anyone in hell is there because of his own choices.

There are many movements that do not believe in a literal hell. The Bible teaches, however, that it is appointed unto man <u>once</u> to die and after that, the judgment (**Heb. 9:27**). Jesus said that hell is a literal place with fire that will burn forever (**Mark 9:43-48**; **Luke 16:19-26**). He also said that hell originally was prepared for the devil and his angels, and that it is not God's will that any human being should go there (**Matthew 25:41**).

Christ Unlimited — P.O. Box 850 — Dewey, AZ 86327   USA

This lake of fire, called <u>Gehenna</u> in the Greek, has no one in it as yet, but is the final destination of all of the damned. Today, the souls of the wicked dead are in <u>Hades</u> (Greek) or <u>Sheol</u> (Hebrew), which is Hell.

The <u>King James Version</u> of the Bible also uses the English word <u>hell</u> for "the grave," "the pit," and "the place of the dead" (**Ps. 16:10**). <u>Hades</u> is not the lake of fire, but a place under the earth where the wicked dead are held pending final judgment. It is something like jail cells for prisoners awaiting sentencing, only of course, that area does not resemble earthly jail cells. Those who are there already know they are in Hell, and they know worse awaits.

Hades is also described as "the deep," "a place beneath the sea," and "the nether world below the surface of the earth" (**Num. 16:30; Ps. 55:15**). Hell has "gates" and "bars" that hold its prisoners. It is described as a place of shame, remorse, full consciousness, memory of life on earth, and anguish for lost opportunities.

At one time, there was a region in Hades, called "Paradise," which was <u>not</u> for the wicked dead. <u>Paradise</u> simply means "a garden of God." Paradise was a place where the <u>righteous dead</u> went prior to Calvary (**Luke 23:43**). Referred to by Jesus as "Abraham's Bosom," it was separated from Hell's lower regions by a great, impassable gulf. Paradise held all of the saints who died before Jesus went to the cross to pay the price for their sins. They could not enter heaven until legally their sins were dealt with on the cross.

Christ Unlimited — P.O. Box 850 — Dewey, AZ 86327   USA

On the cross, Jesus said to the thief who accepted and defended Him, "Today, you will be with Me in Paradise" (Luke 23:43). Until Jesus paid the price on the cross for the salvation of all who would receive Him, not even the righteous dead could stand in the presence of God. After He died and while He was in "the bowels of the earth" three days and three nights, He preached to those who lived before the flood (1 Pet. 3:19,20) and led all of the righteous dead to Heaven (Eph. 4:8-10). Since that time, every person who has received Jesus on earth goes directly to Heaven (2 Corinthians 5:8).

Today, the "gates" of Hell do not prevail against the Church, as they once did against the Old Testament saints (Matt. 16:18). Gates in the Bible symbolize "authority." In the cities of Israel, the civil authorities and leaders sat at the gates to hold court and judge the affairs of the area (Ruth 4:10,11). During his rebellion, David's son Absalom reverted to this practice and substituted judging at the city gate for his father in the palace (2 Samuel 15:2-6).

The "gates" of Hell mean the authorities and powers of Satan who can no longer prevail against God's people. Christ now has the keys to death and Hell (Hades), which ultimately will have to give up its wicked dead for judgment (Rev. 1:18). At that time, unsaved souls will be cast with the devil and his followers into the lake of fire and forever suffer in the flames of Gehenna (Revelation 20:10-15).

By recognizing cults and occult groups, we can steer clear of personal involvement in them. Also, we can pray against the demonic spirits that hold people captive in these organizations and movements. We need to show the love of God to these people, and ask the Holy Spirit how best to witness to them, so that they do not end up in Hell for eternity.

Lesson for Section Three

[Author's Note: Please read pages 20-32, of <u>Exposing Satan's Devices</u>, also the introduction to this section, before beginning this lesson.]

I. Satan's Religions: The Occult

Satan uses the occult to ensnare and deceive many.

A. Occult groups offer supernatural power to their followers

by _____ the gifts of the Holy

Spirit and the true worship of God.

Reference:

Even him, whose coming is after the working of Satan with all power and signs and lying wonders, And with all deceivableness of unrighteousness in them that perish; because they received not the love of the truth, that they might be saved. And for this cause God shall send them strong delusion, that they should believe a lie.

2 Thessalonians 2:9-11

B. The word <u>occult</u> means _____;
therefore, the devil — the master ruler of darkness — uses occultism to involve people with the _____ works of darkness.

Christ Unlimited — P.O. Box 850 — Dewey, AZ 86327   USA

And have no fellowship with the unfruitful works of darkness, but rather reprove them. For it is a shame even to speak of those things which are done of them in secret.

Ephesians 5:11,12

Other reference: Ephesians 6:12

C. The occult practices hidden things of darkness and promotes _____ of _____. There never has been a time in history when the warnings against the dangers of occultism were more necessary than at present.

Now the Spirit speaketh expressly, that in the latter times some shall depart from the faith, giving heed to seducing spirits, and doctrines of devils.

1 Timothy 4:1

D. Multitudes of people, saved and unsaved, have become involved in the diabolical web of occultism, which is under the _____ and _____ of powers of darkness. Many of these people are suffering physical, mental, emotional, and spiritual problems with no idea why.

E. Any involvement with the occult causes one to commit spiritual adultery, or another name for this is _____. Wherefore, my dearly beloved, flee from idolatry.

1 Corinthians 10:14

Examples of idolatry and its consequences are:

Now the works of the flesh are manifest, which are these; Adultery, fornication, uncleanness, lasciviousness, idolatry, witchcraft, hatred, variance, emulations, wrath, strife, seditions, heresies, envyings, murders, drunkenness, revellings and such like: of the which I tell you before, as I have also told you in time past, that they which do such things shall not inherit the kingdom of God.

Galatians 5:19-21

There shall not be found among you any one that maketh his son or his daughter to pass through the fire, or that useth divination, or an observer of times, or an enchanter, or a witch, or a charmer, or a consulter with familiar spirits, or a wizard, or a necromancer. For all that do these things are an abomination unto the Lord.

Deuteronomy 18:10-12

But the fearful, and unbelieving, and the abominable, and murderers, and whoremongers, and sorcerers, and idolaters, and all liars, shall have their part in the lake which burneth with fire and brimstone: which is the second death.

Revelation 21:8

And the soul that turneth after such as have familiar spirits, and after wizards, to go a whoring after them, I will even set my face against that soul, and will cut him off from among his people.

Leviticus 20:6

A partial list of abominations found in Deuteronomy 18:10-15 includes: Divination, witchcraft, astrology, wizardry, consulting with familiar spirits, a necromancer (talking with the dead, a "spiritist" or spiritualism), and an enchanter.

(Also, see page 21 of <u>Exposing Satan's Devices</u> for a list of occult practices.)

F. Involvement in the occult is disobedience to God's word and brings a _____ upon those who pursue it.

The graven images of their gods shall ye burn with fire: thou shalt not desire the silver or gold that is on them, nor take it unto thee, lest thou be snared therein: for it is an abomination to the Lord thy God. Neither shalt thou bring an abomination into thine house, lest thou shalt be a cursed thing like it: but thou shalt utterly detest it, and thou shalt utterly abhor it; for it is a cursed thing.

Christ Unlimited — P.O. Box 850 — Dewey, AZ 86327   USA

And thou shalt not go aside from any of the words which I command thee this day, to the right hand, or to the left, to go after other gods to serve them. But it shall come to pass, <u>if thou wilt not hearken</u> unto the voice of the Lord thy God, to observe to do all his commandments and his statutes which I command thee this day; <u>that all these curses</u> shall come upon thee, and overtake thee.

> Deuteronomy 7:25,26, 28:14,15

G. What are some of the occult practices mentioned in the Bible?

_____

_____

_____

References:

Deuteronomy 7:25, 18:10-15; Leviticus 19:28,31; Hosea 4:12; Isaiah 8:19-20, 47:12-14; Acts 19:18-20

H. List at least three modern-day occult practices:

1. _____

2. _____

3. _____

I. What are some of the marks of cults and occultism?

   1. Denial of Jesus as _____ of the world.

      Reference: **2 Peter 2:1-3**

   2. What is the Christian's definition of Jesus?

      a. Jesus is truly _____.

      b. Jesus also is truly _____.

      c. Jesus was born of a _____.

      d. Jesus shed His _____ for the sins of the world.

      e. Jesus was _____ from the dead.

      f. Jesus will return _____ at His Second Coming.

      g. Jesus is the only begotten _____.

      h. Jesus is _____ today, seated at the right
        hand of the Father.

J. Cults and occult groups refer to God and the Savior in such vague terms as:

   1. _____

   2. _____

   3. _____

   4. _____

   5. _____

   6. _____

II. Cultic Religions' Views of Hell

A. Views on hell are one earmark of cultic religions that:

1. Try to use the _____ of going to Hell to bring people into bondage.

2. Try to discount hell _____.

3. Try to convince people that Hell is on earth, so they should not worry about the _____.

4. Try to get people to believe in _____ at death instead of Hell.

5. Try to teach that Hell is not _____, but only temporary.

6. Try to teach that souls in Hell are _____.

7. Try to teach a _____ for salvation after death, such as in reincarnation.

8. Try to teach that Hell is only _____ from God rather than a literal burning in a fiery lake.

B. What does the Bible say about Hell?

1. Hell originally was prepared for the _____ and _____.

   Reference: Matthew 25:41

2. Jesus said Hell is a place where the _____ does not die, and the fire is never _____.

   References: Mark 9:43-48; Luke 16:19-26

3. The Greek word for Hell in the New Testament is _____,
   which means the same as _____, the Hebrew word
   used in the Old Testament.

4. Hell is spoken of as the _____. Other names are:

   a. _____

   b. _____

   c. It is described as below the surface of the earth,
      beneath the sea, and as the _____.
      References: Numbers 16:30, Psalm 55:15

5. Hell has _____ and _____ that hold its
   prisoners.

6. The wicked go down into the region of Hell, where they are
   kept until the _____.

7. Emotions (feelings) like these, still exist in Hell:

   a. _____

   b. _____

   c. _____

   d. _____

   e. _____

   f. _____

8. Before the resurrection of Jesus, there was a section of
   Hades called _____, where the righteous
   dead went.

Christ Unlimited — P.O. Box 850 — Dewey, AZ 86327   USA

a. Paradise was separated from the region of the damned
   by a _____.

b. Paradise was referred to by Jesus as _____.

c. Abraham and all of the Old Testament saints were kept
   there until Christ's death, burial and _____.

   1) Jesus then descended into Hades and, at His
      ascension, He led "_____."

   2) He _____ the prisoners of hope from
      Paradise and led them to Heaven.

      References: **Psalm 16:10; Luke 23:43;**

      Ephesians 4:8-10

d. Today, the _____ of _____ do not prevail
   against the Church, as they did against the righteous in
   Old Testament days.

   Reference:

And I say also unto thee, That thou art Peter, and upon
this rock I will build my church; and the gates of hell
shall not prevail against it.

                              Matthew 16:18

e. Today, all true believers go directly to _____
   at death and no longer must wait in <u>Paradise</u> as the
   Old Testament saints did.

f. Christ has the keys to _____ and _____

which will give up its wicked dead at the Judgment.

1) Hell then will come to an end, in the _____

of _____ where souls will burn with no escape.

2) That is the second _____.

Reference: Revelation 1:18, 20:10-15

We are confident, I say, and willing rather to be absent

from the body, and to be present with the Lord.

2 Corinthians 5:8

III. Marks of Cults:

A. Leadership that heap _____ upon themselves and

are egocentric.

1. These evil men enslave their followers three ways:

a. _____

b. _____

c. _____

2. Slavery and devotion to _____ is usually a

requirement for membership.

B. Another red flag to watch for as a sign of false cults

is the promise of _____ to members of

the group.

(Leaders of cults tend to talk in long discourses, ask many questions, but provide no real answers. Their speech is mere "circumlocution".)

C. Cult leaders are seldom clear in their definitions or explanations and frequently change their beliefs and rules to adapt to continued doctrinal alterations, such as:

   1. A misplaced emphasis on a _____ of God's Word, which becomes the "test" of <u>true</u> Christianity to them.

   2. They also consider people who do not _____ their doctrine as being unsaved.

D. Cults also try to separate the _____, _____, and _____, with one part of man being "good" and another "bad," thus allowing sin since they say the spirit is not responsible for the body's actions.

E. Extreme _____ is a mark of many cults, although other groups go to the other extreme and say "anything is okay as long as it does not hurt anyone else."

Woe unto you, scribes and Pharisees, hypocrites! for ye pay tithe of mint and anise and cummin, and have omitted the weightier matters of the law, judgment, mercy, and faith: these ought ye to have done, and not to leave the other undone.

Matthew 23:23

Christ Unlimited — P.O. Box 850 — Dewey, AZ 86327   USA

IV. God's Leadership Versus Satan's Control

    A. God's method of leadership is to guide us with _____

       and _____.

    B. Satan controls with _____ and _____.

       References:

I am the good shepherd: the good shepherd giveth his life for the sheep.

                                     John 10:11

Feed the flock of God which is among you, taking oversight thereof, not by constraint, but willingly; not for filthy lucre, but of a ready mind; neither as being lords over God's heritage, but being ensamples to the flock.

                                   1 Peter 5:2,3

For God hath not given us the spirit of fear; but of power, and of love, and of a sound mind.

                                   2 Timothy 1:7

Ye are bought with a price; be not ye the servants of men.

                                1 Corinthians 7:23

Now the Lord is that Spirit: and where the Spirit of the Lord is, there is liberty.

                                2 Corinthians 3:17

Christ Unlimited — P.O. Box 850 — Dewey, AZ 86327   USA

Overcoming Life Memory Verse

The suggested memory verse for this lesson is:

For God hath not given us the spirit of fear; but of power and of love, and of a sound mind.

2 Timothy 1:7

Review Outline, Section Three

[Author's Note: This outline covers pp. 20-32 of <u>Exposing Satan's Devices</u>.]

I. False Religions and Cults (1 Timothy 4:1,2)

   A. False, or counterfeit, doctrines teach:

      1. There are many paths to Heaven.

      2. There is no Hell.

      3. Doctrines that add to or take away from the Word.

   B. They focus on people as powerful leaders, instead of the Holy Spirit.

      1. Churches and Christians should be warned in this one area: not to make "stars" out of their spiritual leaders.

      2. They should be honored and respected, but not given undue praise and glory.

   C. Christian behavior toward cult members is that we are to:

      1. Pray for them.

      2. Love them.

      3. Seek the Holy Spirit on how to reveal truth to them.

II. Occultism Versus Christianity

   A. Occultism mimics the gifts of God and the Holy Spirit (Matthew 24:24).

   B. Occultism operates in practices of darkness.

Christ Unlimited — P.O. Box 850 — Dewey, AZ 86327   USA

C. Occultism promotes damnable doctrines as spoken of in
2 Peter 2:1-3, such as:

1. Demons to be "spirit guides."

2. Satanic power for "magic" charms and witchcraft.

3. Contacting spiritual entities (spiritism).

4. The use of human beings as "mediums" or "channels"
through which these demons and entities can manifest in
the earth.

5. Counterfeit gifts of the Spirit, such as divination instead
of prophecy, extrasensory perception (ESP) instead of
words of wisdom and knowledge; and psychic healing
instead of healing through the blood of Jesus.

D. Participation brings evil and curses on members of these
groups (Isaiah 47:11-14).

Review Outline Quiz, Section Three

1. How many "paths" are there to Heaven?

   _____

2. How do we know there is a Hell?

   _____

3. What are some of the occult practices with which we are familiar today?

   _____

4. What are spirit guides?

   _____

5. What are mediums?

   _____

   _____

6. Christians should not make _____ out of leaders.

7. Occultism mimics _____.

8. We should _____ and _____ for members of cults.

9. Occultism operates in _____ of things of God.

10. Participating in occultism brings _____ and _____.

Christ Unlimited — P.O. Box 850 — Dewey, AZ 86327   USA

Exposing Satan's Devices Workbook

Section Four

"Satanic Deception: Objects and Idols"

Christ Unlimited — P.O. Box 850 — Dewey, AZ 86327   USA

Exposing Satan's Devices Workbook
Section Four: "Satanic Deception: Objects and Idols"
Expository Introduction

The focus in this section is on objects used by cults and occult groups that have an effect on people who possess them.

Demons inhabit objects used in cult and occult practices. When we allow such objects into our homes, even if we are not actively involved in the practices, it brings a curse into our houses (**Deut. 7:25,26**). Many people have such objects as souvenirs, antiquities, artifacts of other cultures, or even religious shrines.

Most people think such things are simply art or curios and harmless. Some of these include statues of Buddha, Indian gods and goddesses, African or Hawaiian masks; Chinese paintings, drawings, or "good luck" artwork with so-called "blessings" on them; voodoo dolls; dragons or unicorns; even such things as collections of animal objects that become an obsession (owls, frogs, and snakes are the most common).

Here are two examples of problems that cleared up, when these types of objects were removed from the people's homes:

*One woman, who had serious back problems, could not receive her healing until she removed a statue of Buddha that was in her home. She was deceived in that she had it in her living room as a decorator item to go with her Chinese furnishings.

Christ Unlimited — P.O. Box 850 — Dewey, AZ 86327   USA

*A mother saw her son become less rebellious once a ceramic snake, a cobra, in his room was destroyed. Many families have reported much less problems with their teenagers once rock music shirts, posters, and albums, cassettes, or CDs were removed from the house.

Other cursed objects include American Indian items of witch-craft:

"God's eyes" made with yarn that represents the medicine man's watchful eye; replicas, paintings, or drawings of birds or animals that have been revered as "totems" for certain tribes, especially the Thunderbird, a mythical "sacred" bird for several tribes; totem poles; the squash blossom, a fertility symbol with a pendant shaped like a half-moon; wood masks, usually of owls, whose spirits are supposed to be guardians of the night; and certain Indian baskets.

The most obviously satanic, however, are dolls that thousands of Christians in the West and Southwest have in their homes and offices: These are called "Kachina dolls." They really are idols, because they are statues and representations of actual demonic figures worshiped by Native Americans.

The Israelites became involved in the demonic through socializing with pagan peoples, which had been forbidden. They even had designs of pagan gods on woven rugs and tapestries in their homes. (2 Kings 23:7). Sometimes, they actually possessed statues of those gods and goddesses.

Pennsylvania Dutch "hex" signs and some weather artifacts off the tops of old barns are really witchcraft symbols.

Christ Unlimited — P.O. Box 850 — Dewey, AZ 86327   USA

Also, there are "games" today that are very popular but actually are satanic. The Ouija board is an openly occult game that has been popular for about a hundred years. Such modern games include Dungeons and Dragons and some computer games such as "Doom." Pendulum games also are satanic.

Witchcraft That Appears "Good"

Demons can inhabit certain pieces of jewelry with occult objects as pendants or charms. Emblems such as the Egyptian ankh, the "peace sign" (which really is the "broken cross" and mocks Jesus' death), and the horn of plenty that looks like a tooth and is supposed to bring good luck, but actually brings a financial curse.

Other jewelry items popular today that are of demonic origin include mood rings and items with the unicorn symbol. The <u>unicorn</u> is a witchcraft symbol that is supposed to also govern finances.

Another popular symbol, particularly used by Christians today, is the so-called "Star of David." As the emblem of a nation which is our main ally in the Middle East, it is a political symbol like the Stars and Stripes. However, contrary to what many Christians believe, it is not a Biblical symbol, and the "David" is not the David of the Bible but a political "messiah" of the Jewish people about the 1300s. (Any Jewish reference book on religious symbols or encyclopedia gives the <u>facts</u> about this symbol.)

Christians have made an assumption, because of prophetic doctrines concerning the modern nation of Israel, that this symbol goes back to King David and the tribe of Judah. Most of them have made no effort to research the origin of this "star," which actually is the same <u>hexagram</u> used in black masses to honor Satan.

The average dictionary defines the "Star of David" as a political symbol of Judaism (which, today, without Jesus as its focus, is as "false" a religion) and also as a "mystic" symbol from the Middle Ages, called "Solomon's Seal." The tribe of Judah's symbol in the Bible is the <u>lion</u>, not a star (**Gen. 49:9**). That is why Jesus is called "the Lion of the Tribe of Judah" (**Revelation 5:5**).

Another form of satanism and witchcraft comes into people's homes through popular music. "Heavy metal" is the worst, with rock music being next. However, even country music and jazz can bring demonic influences into a house, depending on the beat of the music and the particular lyrics. The records, cassettes, or CDs of the openly demonic songs have an evil Satanic anointing on them which influences the minds and emotions of the listeners.

Even so-called Christian-rock or "Jesus rock" is destructive, since the beat of the music has its origin in witchcraft and satanism.

Other forms of entertainment that are satanic in origin today include many children's toys (He-man and Teenage Mutant Ninja Turtles are at the top of these), most science-fiction movies, television programs that promote witchcraft, horror books and films, vampires and witch films and books, and most fantasy books and films.

Any occult or New Age films, books, or music are satanically influenced, and some are actively inhabited by demons. Most New Age music today is marketed as meditation or mood elevation sounds that are not always labeled "New Age." Sometimes on the surface, it seems nice, gentle, soothing music — with heavy overtones of nature sounds. However, its origin is from the "spirit world" and from "guides" who give false inspiration. Not all "sights and sounds" music is from the wrong source. We must pray for God's discernment about this. In fact, Christians must be discerning in all areas of their lives.

Another danger in the music and tape realm is the so-called "subliminal" messages designed to help people overcome certain problems in their lives. These are supposed to help people lose weight and conquer other bad habits through recorded messages that cannot be heard with the natural ear, but supposedly are designed to influence the subconscious mind, bringing about needed change as the message is geared for positive confessions. (An example would be: "I am slim; I am not hungry," for the weight-loss subliminal tape.)

Now there are even subliminal tapes supposedly designed to help Christians hear the Word of God through these messages, bringing a positive influence into their lives. The danger and problem with these tapes is that the listener is open and vulnerable to believing and accepting what the manufacturer <u>says</u> is recorded in the hidden messages. The listener has no way of knowing for sure,

Christ Unlimited — P.O. Box 850 — Dewey, AZ 86327   USA

because the subconscious mind is receiving the message while the natural ear only hears music or surface messages.

Personally, I have a hard time believing God would use these messages in order for us to be relieved of the discipline of studying and memorizing the Word, as Scripture admonishes us to do.

> And be not conformed to this world: but be ye transformed by the renewing of your mind, that ye may prove what is that good, and acceptable, and perfect, will of God.
>
> Romans 12:2
>
> Let no man deceive you with vain words: for because of these things cometh the wrath of God upon the children of disobedience.
>
> Ephesians 5:6

> Study to show thyself approved unto God, a workman that needeth not to be ashamed, rightly dividing the word of truth.
>
> 2 Timothy 2:15

These scriptures tell us that our conscious minds are actively involved in the process of sanctification. So, at best, these tapes are a waste of time, and at worst, they could carry a destructive anointing from Satan to ensnare people.

Also, as Christians, we should avoid the use of certain phrases, such as "I'm lucky," or "I always have bad luck," "She makes me sick," "I'm dying to go," "That frightens me," or "I could kill them." Any words that are negative or use witchcraft phraseology should be avoided.

There Is No Such Thing as <u>Luck</u>.

Circumstances and situations that occur in our lives are the result of the keeping or breaking of certain spiritual laws by us or others that affect our lives.

I call heaven and earth to record this day against you, that I have set before you life and death, blessing and cursing: therefore choose life, that both thou and thy seed may live.

Deuteronomy 30:19

. . . The curse causeless shall not come.

Proverbs 26:2

Not "luck," but our own choices and actions affect our futures.

Saying someone has "bad or good vibes" is using New Age terminology. They put a lot of credence on the vibrations from someone's "aura" (supposed fields of color around each person that represent their personalities.)

Also, one very wicked holiday that Satan uses ensnares many deceived Christians. It is Halloween, or All Hallow's Eve, a satanic holiday that Christians should avoid celebrating in any way. The very decorations that go with it shows that Halloween celebrates evil:

witches on broomsticks, goblins, devils, and weird masks. Dressing our children in evil outfits can also attract demons to them.

In addition to avoiding these things, there are several steps we can take to overcome the power of darkness behind cursed objects and cleanse any curses out of our lives.

*First, destroy by crushing or burning any objects representing a curse. Do not simply throw them away and, certainly, do not sell them to someone else even in a garage or yard sale. Even if those objects have been expensive, do not save them from destruction. Christians should discard all albums, cassettes, CDs, posters, T-shirts, and anything else that represents this form of witchcraft (Eph. 4:27).

Read Acts 19:19 to see what the apostles had people do with such things. In recent years, a Texas evangelist was given priceless art objects, statues of pagan gods in silver and gold, and other such things valued at more than $1 million. Although his ministry could have used the money, he made newspaper headlines across the country by smashing and burning all those things. The millionaire who had given them to him had become born again and later helped him destroy those objects.

*Repent of any such involvement with the occult arts and witch-craft, even if it was unintentional or out of ignorance.

*Cast out any evil spirits that entered our homes through such objects, and invite the Holy Spirit to cleanse us from any and every curse the objects brought to us or our homes.

Concerning demons, however, we want to be careful not to fall into either of two extremes: Seeing demons in everything and everyone or refusing to believe demons can influence or inhabit Christians or their homes. We need to maintain a balanced approach.

Can a Christian Have a Demon?

To answer scripturally whether Christians can "have a demon", first look at the personalities of demons. They walk, hear, speak, see, obey, seek, think, and have knowledge. They are spirit beings invisible to the natural eye, as are God's angels. In other words, they are <u>real</u>, and they can dwell in the bodies of people or animals (Matthew 12:43-45; Mark 1:23,24,3:11).

Evil spirits look for a person in which to dwell in order to hide themselves, blending into the person's mind, emotions, or body so that they seem to that person as a natural part of his, or her, personality. Although these spirits are under Satan's jurisdiction, they are subject to Christ and to any of His followers, <u>who will exercise authority in His name and through His blood</u>.

The name of Jesus and the Holy Spirit hold power over them. If we truly allow the Holy Spirit to have full authority over us, demons cannot harm us. Part of the Great Commission to Christians (**Mark 16:15-18**) indicates that demonic oppression or possession is not a rare, isolated phenomenon since the disciples were instructed to cast out demons wherever they went.

There are two main sources for problems in a Christian's life: the flesh (Rom. 8:5-8) and demons. We get victory over the flesh by "crucifying" it (Gal. 5:24). Yes, a Christian can have a demon or have a demonic problem. We get victory over demons by "casting them out" through spiritual warfare.

Part of our cleansing includes being cleansed of any filthiness of spirit (2 Cor. 7:1). If we are disobedient to God, demonic spirits can work in us, causing a defilment in our human spirits (Eph. 2:2). Not only can Christians have demons, but so can their children (Mark 9:20-22).

There are three main identifying marks of evil spirits:

*Addictions, compulsions, or obsessions — anything a person has great difficulty controlling by will power.

*Defilement — acts committed by demonic encouragement and evil or mean words spoken against a person by himself or against someone else that he regrets but cannot seem to help.

*Torment, or continual harassment of the mind.

If a person has renounced evil and committed his life to Christ, yet has not found peace and victory, any problems are likely to be due to demonic influence. The need for deliverance is quite common (Mark 1:22-27; Luke 10:1-17; Mark 16:15-19). Deliverance was common in first-century ministries like those of Peter, Paul, and Philip (Acts 8:6,8, 5:16). The solution to a demonic problem is to have the source cast out (Mark 16:17). Discerning of spirits (1 Cor.

Christ Unlimited — P.O. Box 850 — Dewey, AZ 86327   USA

12:10) is a gift of the Holy Spirit to the Body of Christ that enables Christians to better recognize and cast out demons. For example, when prayer for healing seems ineffective, more than likely a spirit of infirmity needs to be cast off or out of the person.

To answer, "Can a Christian be demon-possessed", we need to understand the meaning of the word <u>possession</u>. No, a Christian cannot be totally possessed and still be a Christian. However, possession comes by degrees and Satan's plan is to try to get Christians to forsake God and ultimately lose their salvation. He begins the process by tempting man to sin and then attaching a demon to the sin area which then opens the door for more sin, demons, and evil with man's total destruction as his goal.

The most common misunderstanding that hinders Christians from believing they can have a demon is usage of the term, "demon possession." They immediately think of the Gadarene demoniac in Matthew 8, who was so possessed of devils that he was in chains and insane.

<u>Possession</u> does not necessarily mean one is filled with demons and completely taken over. People who have been taken over by demons are the ones we refer to as having "lost their minds," as insane, or as having mental problems. Mental institutions are filled with demons feeding off inmates and manipulating some of them under full control. By definition, <u>possession</u> means "ownership," or "having control over something."

Christ Unlimited — P.O. Box 850 — Dewey, AZ 86327   USA

Possession Is Progressive

Possession generally occurs by degrees. When a demon gets a place in someone's life, he calls in others and progressively takes more and more territory. <u>A Christian cannot be totally possessed</u>. If he were, that would mean Satan had full control of the person — spirit, soul, and body; therefore, the person would no longer be a Christian. However, Satan <u>may</u> gain control in, or possession of, certain areas of a Christian's life. Demons try to gain more and more control from whatever foothold (stronghold) they can get. Satan's goal is to get Christians to forsake God and to blaspheme the Holy Spirit, thereby losing their inheritance. But Jesus came to set us free (Luke 4:18)!

Instead of the Church arguing over whether a Christian can be possessed or just oppressed, we should understand that it makes no difference if a demon is on the outside, pushing someone around (oppression), or on the inside leading that person around (possession). The important thing is to identify whether there <u>is</u> a demonic problem, and if so, deal with it.

Total possession does not happen all at once. It is progressive as Satan tries to gain more and more territory in people's lives. Sometimes we are only dealing with one devil, while other people may have numerous demons, but the good news is that deliverance can come all at once! As soon as Jesus spoke to the Gadarene demoniac, the demons left. We have His authority to do the same thing. Jesus allowed the demons to enter the pigs after they left the demoniac to demonstrate the destructive nature of devils. They drove the pigs to death. Demons can drive people to suicide in the same way.

<u>One</u> demon is enough to destroy a person's life and ministry. It does not take total possession to hinder victory for a Christian. If there are problems that do not seem to respond to prayer, or if the promises in the Bible do not seem to be operating, no matter how much a person believes them — that person probably needs some deliverance.

Conditions that must be met in order to gain permanent freedom from demonic bondage are:

*A person must be born again, a true child of God (**John 1:12**).

*That person should have made a verbal confession of faith in the Lord Jesus Christ (**Romans 10:9,10**).

*He needs to acknowledge and confess the sin that gave the devil access to his life. This is where any previous cultic or occultic involvement can be dealt with. If we confess our sins, He is faithful and just to forgive us our sins and to cleanse us from all unrighteousness (**1 John 1:9**).

*The fourth step is to break Satan's legal right over our lives by renouncing each lie the devil used to cause us to sin, and then replacing them with the Word of God (**John 8:32**).

*We should resist the devil <u>out loud</u> and command demons to flee, according to the Word of God (**James 4:7**).

*Caution: the prayer of deliverance should only be carried out by born-again, Spirit-filled believers, who have faith in God's delivering power.

Christ Unlimited — P.O. Box 850 — Dewey, AZ 86327   USA

Lesson for Section Four

[Author's Note: Please read the expository introduction and Chapter Three, pp. 32-49, in Exposing Satan's Devices before taking this lesson.]

I. Demons Inhabit Cultic and Occultic Objects

Reference:

> The graven images of their gods shall ye burn with fire: thou shalt not desire the silver or gold that is on them, nor take it unto thee, lest thou be snared therein: for it is an abomination to the Lord thy God. Neither shalt thou bring an abomination into thine house, lest thou be a cursed thing like it: but thou shalt utterly detest it, and thou shalt utterly abhor it; for it is a cursed thing.
>
> Deuteronomy 7:25,26

A. Some objects or idols are not generally recognized as evil due to the traditions of men.

1. Decorator items, such as:

a. _____

b. _____

c. _____

Christ Unlimited — P.O. Box 850 — Dewey, AZ 86327   USA

2. American Indian witchcraft items, such as:

a. _____

b. _____

c. _____

Reference: Deuteronomy 7:25,26

And he brake down the houses of the sodomites, that were by the house of the Lord, where the women wove hangings for the grove.

2 Kings 23:7

B. Other items that carry demonic oppression include:

1. _____

2. _____

My people ask counsel at their stocks, and their staff declareth unto them: for the spirit of whoredoms hath caused them to err, and they have gone a whoring from under their God.

Hosea 4:12

I will set no wicked thing before mine eyes: I hate the work of them that turn aside; it shall not cleave to me.

Psalm 101:3

3. Jewelry with pendants, such as the _____.

4. Another form of witchcraft comes through _____ music. Tapes, albums, and videos are one of the greatest evils in young people's lives. That includes so-called "Jesus rock." Other music that can be destructive includes:

a. _____

b. _____

c. _____

Neither give place to the devil.

Ephesians 4:27

5. Some of the science-fiction movies and television programs and computer games that promote witchcraft, horror themes, and psychic phenomenon include:

a. _____

b. _____

c. _____

d. _____

e. _____

Christ Unlimited — P.O. Box 850 — Dewey, AZ 86327   USA

But in his estate shall he honour the God of forces: and a god whom his fathers knew not shall he honour with gold, and silver, and with precious stones, and pleasant things.

Daniel 11:38

6. The objects we have revealed as being satanic, along with any books or games that have occult or demonic themes should be _____.

   (This applies particularly to any books or games on reincarnation, transcendental meditation, science of mind, and works by such well-known occult and New Age writers as Edgar Cayce and Jean Dixon.)

And many that believed came, and confessed, and shewed their deeds. Many of them also which used curious arts brought their books together, and burned them before all men: and they counted the price of them, and found it fifty thousand pieces of silver.

Acts 19:18,19

7. Words we should avoid that are not of faith include such expressions as:

   a. _____

   b. _____

   c. _____

Christ Unlimited — P.O. Box 850 — Dewey, AZ 86327   USA

d. _____

e. _____

Nor should we carry good-luck charms such as rabbit's feet.

Reference: Ephesians 5:4-12

II. How Can We Overcome the Powers of Darkness?

A. _____

B. _____

C. _____

D. _____

III. Can Demons Dwell in Christians?

A. What are demons?

_____

B. Describe the characteristics of demons:

_____

_____

References: Matthew 12:43-45; Mark 1:23,24, 3:11

C. To whom are they subject?

1. _____

2. _____

3. _____

Christ Unlimited — P.O. Box 850 — Dewey, AZ 86327   USA

And these signs shall follow them that believe; In my name shall they cast out devils; they shall speak with new tongues.

Mark 16:17

D. What two extremes are to be avoided concerning demons?

1. _____

2. _____

E. What are the two main causes of Christians' problems?

1. _____

2. _____

F. Victory is obtained over the flesh by _____ it.

And they that are Christ's have crucified the flesh with the affections and lusts.

Galatians 5:24

Having therefore these promises, dearly beloved, let us cleanse ourselves from all filthiness of the flesh and spirit, perfecting holiness in the fear of God.

2 Corinthians 7:1

Wherein in time past ye walked according to the course of this world, according to the prince of the power of the air, the spirit that now worketh in the children of disobedience.

Ephesians 2:2

But we are bound to give thanks alway to God for you, brethren beloved of the Lord, because God hath from the beginning chosen you to salvation through sanctification of the Spirit and belief of the truth.

2 Thessalonians 2:13

Also, read Matthew 12:43-45.

G. Christians can have demons, and so can their _____.

And they brought him (a young boy) unto him (Jesus): and when he saw him, straightway the spirit tare him; and he fell on the ground, and wallowed foaming. And he (Jesus) asked his father, How long is it ago since this came unto him? And he said, Of a child. And ofttimes it hath cast him into the fire and into the waters, to destroy him: but if thou canst do any thing, have compassion on us, and help us.

Mark 9:20-22

H. The three main identifying marks of evil spirits are:

1. _____

2. _____

3. _____

I. If a person has renounced evil and committed his life to Christ, but still has not found peace and victory, the problem very likely is due to the influence of evil spirits. The need for _____ is common and should not be viewed as freakish or out-of-the-ordinary.
References: Mark 1:22-27; Luke 10:1-17; Mark 16:15-19

   1. Deliverance was _____ in early Church ministries.

   2. Name two apostles who had such ministries.

      a. _____

      b. _____

   References: Acts 5:16, 8:6,7

J. The solution to the demon problem is to have the demon

_____   _____.

Reference: Mark 16:17

   a. _____ of _____ is a gift of the Holy Spirit that accompanies "casting out" of demons.

   b. A spirit of _____ must sometimes be dealt with when prayer for healing does not suffice.

And, behold, there was a woman which had a spirit of infirmity eighteen years, and was bowed together, and could in no wise lift up herself. And when Jesus saw her, he called her to him, and said unto her, Woman, thou art loosed from thine infirmity. And he laid his hands on her: and immediately she was made straight, and glorified God.

Luke 13:11-13

Jesus healed this woman on the Sabbath Day, at which the Pharisees criticized Him, but He said:

And ought not this woman, being a daughter of Abraham, whom Satan hath bound, lo, these eighteen years, be loosed from this bond on the sabbath day?

Luke 13:16

K. Can a Christian be totally possessed? _____

A Christian can be possessed only if he chooses to follow Satan literally or in deeds and renounces Jesus. At that point of blaspheming the Holy Spirit, the person no longer is a Christian. Total possession requires surrender of the will. The Greek word translated *possession* means "to hold." So, anyone who is out of control in an area, Satan is said to have a "stronghold" there. The person has lost control, and a demon is holding that person captive. However, he is not totally possessed until he surrenders his spirit, soul, and body.

Christ Unlimited — P.O. Box 850 — Dewey, AZ 86327   USA

1. Satan's plan is to bring people to the place of total possession by progressively taking more and more _____ in their lives.

2. Jesus came to set the _____ free.
   Reference: Matthew 12:22

The Spirit of the Lord is upon me, because he hath anointed me to preach the gospel to the poor; he hath sent me to heal the brokenhearted, to preach deliverance to the captives, and recovering of sight to the blind, to set at liberty them that are bruised.

Luke 4:18

3. When a demon is on the outside, pushing someone around it is said to be _____ them. If it is on the inside leading them, it is said to be _____ them. It really does not matter whether the demon is inside or outside, it should be dealt with to get the person free.

4. Someone who continues to sin gives the devil a stronger and stronger hold in his, or her, life. This possession occurs slowly by _____.

   a. Possession does not necessarily mean one is _____ with demons and completely out of control.
   b. Possession has such a derogatory meaning to us,

because of the Bible story about the_____.

Reference: Luke 8:26-36

c. Why did Jesus allow the demons to enter the pigs?

_____

d. How many demons does it take to destroy a person's

life? _____

e. What kind of people are totally possessed today?

_____

L. What conditions must be met in order to gain permanent

deliverance from demonic bondage?

1. _____

But as many as received him, to them gave he power to become the sons of God, even to them that believe on his name.

John 1:12

2. _____

That if thou shalt confess with thy mouth the Lord Jesus, and shalt believe in thine heart that God hath raised him from the dead, thou shalt be saved. For with the heart man believeth unto righteousness; and with the mouth confession is made unto salvation.

Romans 10:9,10

3. _____

If we confess our sins, he is faithful and just to forgive us our sins, and to cleanse us from all unrighteousness.

1 John 1:9

4. _____

_____

And ye shall know the truth, and the truth shall make you free.

John 8:32

5. _____

Submit yourselves therefore to God. Resist the devil, and he will flee from you.

James 4:7

M. Who are the only ones who should pray for deliverance for those who have demonic problems?

_____

_____

References: Mark 16:15-18; Acts 19:13-16

Christ Unlimited — P.O. Box 850 — Dewey, AZ 86327   USA

Lest Satan should get an advantage of us: for we are not ignorant of his devices.

                              2 Corinthians 2:11

For we wrestle not against flesh and blood, but against principalities, against powers, against the rulers of the darkness of this world, against spiritual wickedness in high places.

                              Ephesians 6:12

Overcoming Life Memory Verse

The suggested memory verse for this lesson is:

Submit yourselves therefore to God. Resist the devil, and he will flee from you.

                              James 4:7

Review Outline, Section Four

[**Author's Note**: This outline is based on pp. 26-65 of <u>Exposing Satan's Devices</u>.]

I. Overcoming Satan's Plans

  A. Victory in Christ

    1. Jesus' death, descent, and ascension defeated the enemy (**Ephesians 4:8-10**).

    2. He delivered the righteous dead from Paradise to Heaven, and atoned for all believers with His blood.

  B. In order to walk in victory, seek first the Kingdom of God

    1. Be separate from the world (**John 17:15-17**).

      a. Avoid negative or ungodly speech.

      b. Seek to be a "light" (a blessing) (**Ephesians 5:4-12**).

      c. Avoid fellowship with darkness (**Ephesians 5:11-13**), which is:

        1) Observance of pagan ways, such as Halloween and some of our Easter and Christmas customs and traditions that set up "Santa Claus" or the "Easter bunny" as figures to be honored in place of Christ on these holidays.

        2) Making "gods" of television and movie personalities, opening a home to ungodly music and entertainment

3) Having ungodly things or practices in the home

   (2 Corinthians 7:1), such as:

   (a) Occult decorations (2 Kings 23:7)

   (b) Occult or evil books, music, or videos

      (Acts 19:18,19)

   (c) Certain "habits" can be demonic

   (d) Anti-Christian symbols on clothing, jewelry,

      or art works (Deuteronomy 7:25,26)

   (e) Games of "chance" (gambling)

   (f) Pagan or satanic objects

2. Seek deliverance when necessary (Mark 1:34).

   a. Pray for guidance, and fast to hear God.

   b. Find anointed fellow Christians to pray with.

   c. Renounce and resist any demonic influence.

   d. Look for a church or ministry that operates in
      deliverance.

3. Ways unclean spirits can enter include:

   a. Ungodly practices or associations (Galatians 5:19-21)

   b. Altered states of consciousness and other New Age
      practices and teachings, such as meditation and
      astrology

   c. Generational curses ("chains of iniquity")
      (Jeremiah 32:18,19; Exodus 20:5,6)

II. Overcoming Satan's Curses

    A. Curses may be generational (Deuteronomy 27,28,29; Jeremiah 32:18,19) and can manifest as:

        1. Emotional illnesses

        2. Mental illnesses

        3. Physical illnesses

    B. Curses enter a person or a generational line through:

        1. Sins of various kinds

        2. Disobedience, or being out of God's will

        3. Prayerlessness

        4. Not being in fellowship with God's people

        5. Not studying the Word so that one is ignorant of Satan's devices; in other words, a lack of knowledge (Hosea 4:6)

    C. Curses can be broken by a believer who:

        1. Prays to be forgiven

        2. Repents

        3. Receives the blessings in faith

        4. Prays for any who have cursed him or his family line

        5. Claims Psalm 91 personally

        6. Walks in victory, not fear

        7. Overcomes evil with good

Christ Unlimited — P.O. Box 850 — Dewey, AZ 86327   USA

Review Outline Quiz, Section Four

1. A Christian is automatically protected from demons:

    True _____ False _____

2. Name three ways to be separate from the world.

    a. _____

    b. _____

    c. _____

3. List three ways a Christian can open his life to a curse.

    a. _____

    b. _____

    c. _____

4. Write out a scripture that shows how God protects us from evil.

    _____

    _____

    _____

5a. How can a Christian inherit a curse? _____

_____

5b. What can be done about it? _____

_____

6. Curses can be broken by overcoming _____ with

_____.

7. Name at least one way unclean spirits gain access to a life.

_____

8. How did Jesus overcome Satan and his works?

_____

9. How do generational curses manifest?

_____

10. To obtain victory, seek first _____.

Christ Unlimited — P.O. Box 850 — Dewey, AZ 86327   USA

Exposing Satan's Devices Workbook

Section Five:

"Guidelines for Casting Out Demons"

Exposing Satan's Devices Workbook
Section Five: "Guidelines for Casting Out Demons"
Expository Introduction:

If we are to be overcomers, we need to recognize our enemy in order to be able to stand against him. This lesson will deal specifically with the subject of demons and the Christian's authority over them.

As I have mentioned before, one of the things Christians were told to do in the Great Commission (**Mark 16:15-18**) is cast out demons. Verse 17 of that passage says:

And these signs shall follow them that believe; In my name shall they cast out devils . . .

That is part of the "full gospel" message that we as believers are commissioned to do. Casting out demons in others is not risky, but it requires faith. That is why it should be done only by born-again, Spirit-filled believers. If a person knows that he lacks faith in this area, then he should not try it, but find someone who can help.

If he asks the Holy Spirit, He will direct that person to someone who can pray the prayer of faith. Unbelievers can experience disastrous results if they attempt to cast out demons. In **Acts 19:13-16**, we are told about seven sons of Sceva, the Jewish chief priest in Ephesus, who operated as "exorcists." They had observed the

Apostle Paul casting out demons, so they tried it "in the name of the Jesus Paul preaches."

The demons turned on them, saying, "We know Jesus, and we know Paul — but who are you?"

Then the man in whom the demons lived beat the seven, tore off their clothes, and sent them running down the street! Because these men were not born again, they had no protection from demons. The devil recognizes the authority of Christ in a person as well as he recognizes one who has no faith.

However, if a person has Jesus in him, then he personally knows the Jesus about whom Paul preached and need have no fear of demons.

Sometimes when a Christian first attempts to cast out demons, that person may be "challenged" by the demon. Satan tries to use his weapon of fear to keep Christians from operating in the authority they have in Christ with the ability to cast out demons. The devil may whisper that the demons will attack the person who is praying or do something destructive to that person or his family. Those are lies, and we must not allow the enemy to put fear upon us and intimidate us.

1 John 4:4 says:

Ye are of God, little children, and have overcome them: because greater is he that is in you than he that is in the world.

If we allow fear to overcome us, then we have opened doors to receive spirits of fear. If we have this problem, we need to get help from other believers who are more experienced at dealing with demons. However, if we resist fear and the lies of Satan, we will be free to move in the authority of Jesus' name by the power of the Holy Spirit.

If the level of faith is not where it should be, a time of fasting and prayer can restore it. Jesus' disciples had this problem as recorded in **Matthew 17:14-21**, when they were unable to cast out a devil from a child. Jesus told the disciples that unbelief and lack of faith was the reason they had been unable to cast out the demon. He admonished them to fast and pray to restore their faith.

Fasting and prayer will keep us out of unbelief. When fear tries to creep in, get back into fasting and prayer.

Concerning methods of casting out demons, there is no set rule — except for hearing the Holy Spirit on what to do.

Two things new Christians ask about deliverance are:

1. Should we, or should we not, lay hands on the individual who is receiving the deliverance?

2. Should we plead the blood of Jesus over a person when we cast out demons?

Again, the answer is: There is no hard and fast rule. The thing that is most necessary is <u>to be led by the Spirit</u>. Someone who is totally possessed probably should not have hands laid on him, unless there are a number of strong men to help hold him down.

Demons in a possessed person have total control of his actions and are superhumanly strong. However, in most cases of deliverance, it would be okay to lay hands on the person being prayed for as demons are commanded to come out.

In regard to "pleading the blood of Jesus" during deliverance, there are two extremes people can fall into: one is to ignore the blood altogether, and the other is to treat it as a "magic potion" or a fetish of some sort. We should not make a fetish out of the blood of Jesus. In other words, we must understand its effectiveness and have faith in what Jesus' shed blood accomplished. However, we must keep our eyes on the fact that <u>Jesus</u> has the power and not make speaking about His blood equal with <u>Him</u>.

Just screaming, "You can't cross the bloodline, you can't cross the bloodline," is not effective unless it is done in faith.

Sometimes, it does help in deliverance to remind the demons that Jesus defeated them <u>and</u> their master on the cross through His shed blood. Remind demons that faith in what the blood did for us is what allows us to confidently command them to leave in the <u>name</u> of Jesus.

Some people believe that only the first disciples could cast out demons. However, all Christians since that time are expected to be "disciples." Discipleship simply means someone who is totally committed to God and who patterns his life after Jesus and attempts to follow in His footsteps. In other words, a disciple is someone who is disciplined and obedient to the Word of God.

Another question many people ask is, "If the demons cannot come on us in deliverance, where do they go?"

Where Do Demons Go, and How Do They Act?

Mark 5:10 says they seek another "house," another place to live. Matthew 12:43-45 says that, if they do not find such a place, they wander in "dry places." That means in areas where there is no living being to inhabit. Demons live vicariously through natural life, experiencing through humans or animals the feelings of being alive themselves. Without that, it is "dry" for them. They are simply wandering spirits with no place to go except Hades.

Demons cannot be destroyed, any more than any other eternal spirit being, once they have come into existence. There is much God did not see fit to explain to us in His Word, so we should not speculate beyond what we are told. However, obviously, if spirits could be destroyed, a merciful God would do so rather than leave them alive as potential troublemakers. At this time, they are allowed to roam the earth; however, at Christ's return, the devil and all of his demons will be bound in the pit of hell (Rev. 20). They apparently cannot be destroyed, but God has a plan to contain them, so they no longer torment His people. Jesus came to destroy the <u>works</u> of the devil, not the devil himself, according to 1 John 3:8.

...For this purpose the Son of God was manifested, that he might destroy the works of the devil.

Christ Unlimited — P.O. Box 850 — Dewey, AZ 86327   USA

The eternal destination for all beings, human or angelic, is either Heaven or Hell. Every human being who has ever been born will live forever. The only question is: <u>Where</u> will they spend eternity? Sometimes we hear people say that becoming born again gives us eternal life. No, it does not. We <u>already</u> have eternal life. Being born again provides us with eternal life <u>with God</u>. Everyone lives forever. The only question is where we are going to live. That is the most important thing we can ever settle in this lifetime.

Although we cannot destroy demons, we can:

*Take authority over them.

*Cast them out of people.

*Destroy their works.

*Destroy their influence.

We must be aware, however, that the power of Satan and/or his demons is not <u>automatically</u> overcome by the life of God within our spirits, the presence of Jesus within us, nor even the infilling of the Holy Spirit.

Although, legally, Jesus has accomplished for us on the cross all of our provisions and blessings, which include salvation, healing, atonement, the power to become new creatures, we must do our parts to receive those provisions and blessings. He made a way for us to be blessed for life. However, we must appropriate by faith our covenant blessings and then exercise faith to maintain our positions of authority over Satan and his demons.

When Jesus left earth, He delegated His authority to His Body. As members of that Body, we can — and are expected to — individually exercise that authority, as well as participate in corporate exercises of Jesus' authority. In other words, some things must be done by a church, or by <u>the</u> Church, as a group.

A mature Christian will walk in all of the responsibilities mentioned in the Great Commission. That includes preaching the gospel, casting out demons, speaking with new tongues, and healing the sick, knowing in total faith that, while on the Lord's business, nothing can hurt us.

When we become born again, we usually experience some initial deliverance, because some demons will depart when the Holy Spirit brings God's life into us. However, generally speaking, no one is automatically free from the former satanic hold of the world on one's mind. They must be specifically dealt with in the areas that had been opened to the devil while they were yet unsaved.

We must <u>yield</u> to the Holy Spirit in order for our spirits to be cleansed, and this takes a process of time and growth of spiritual maturity (Colossians 3:5-14; Ephesians 2:2).

Bob Mumford, a spiritual leader and teacher to the Body at large, said once that there are two ways to get rid of devils: Cast them out, or starve them out, meaning do not feed them any more of the things they were "eating" or living on. For example, if someone has a problem with smoking, and that person is being controlled by this

Christ Unlimited — P.O. Box 850 — Dewey, AZ 86327 USA

addiction and a spirit is involved, then he should fast and pray to the point where he can <u>choose</u> against it. When an evil spirit is denied the pleasure it gets from a human's addiction and misery, it will leave for greener pastures.

Indications of Demonic Presences

Demons are not as difficult to get rid of as they are to keep from coming back. Maintaining deliverance requires steadfastness and willpower, because we must deal with the area in the flesh through which the demon entered. We can cast one out in a few seconds, but it takes some time to change our thinking, habits, or attitudes so the demon has no place in us to which he can return.

We must allow the Holy Spirit to fill the void where the demon was; or the Bible says that demon will come back and bring seven others with him, making the state of that person worse than it was before deliverance (**Matthew 12:43-45**).

Some of the demonic manifestations Biblical accounts show us can happen during deliverance because of demonic manifestations include:

*Crying out

*Weeping profusely

*Screaming and cursing

*Falling down as if dead

*Rolling around on the floor or ground; perhaps writhing like a snake

Christ Unlimited — P.O. Box 850 — Dewey, AZ 86327   USA

*Foaming at the mouth, spitting, and vomiting

However, none of these things may occur at all, so do not expect or look for any manifestations during deliverance. Demons can be made to leave without any of these unpleasant things happening. Jesus commanded an unclean devil in a man to hold its peace (quit speaking) and not to hurt the man when He cast it out. The story is told in Luke 4:33-35:

> And in the synagogue there was a man, which had a spirit of an unclean devil, and cried out with a loud voice, Saying, Let us alone; what have we to do with thee, thou Jesus of Nazareth? art thou come to destroy us? I know thee who thou art; the Holy One of God. And Jesus rebuked him, saying, Hold thy peace, and come out of him. And when the devil had thrown him in the midst, he came out of him, and hurt him not.

One thing not to do in deliverance is carry on conversations with the demons! People who do this can come under deception or captivity themselves. Demons are liars as a matter of character, and talking to them gives them a "platform" from which to put forth their lies and ideas. We do not have to know what kind of demon it is before casting it out. We can just command all unclean devils to come out.

If we do need to know, the Holy Spirit will tell us — if we are sensitive to His voice and walking in faith. Here are some indications of demonic presence that we can spot without talking to the demon:

*The person is totally unreasonable about something.

*He displays evidence of a spirit of lust or anger that is abnormal, compulsive, or obsessive. Addictions are definite signs of evil spirits.

*In our minds, if something — a past sin or a picture of some temptation that we really do not want to do — keeps coming back to our minds over and over, that probably is evidence of the presence of a tormenting evil spirit.

*Bondage to another person by abnormal dependency.

The Bible speaks of several different kinds of evil spirits that can be behind sins that seemingly overpower people. These include:

Seducing spirits; spirits that are unclean or foul, perverse, sorrowful, jealous, and anti-Christ; also, spirits of whoredom, bondage, error, divination, and fear. The Bible talks about familiar spirits, deaf and dumb spirits, spirits of infirmities, and others. Looking up the scriptures referring to these evil spirits in a good concordance can throw further enlightenment on demonic activities.

These spirits must be dealt with in the spiritual realm. For example, homosexuals have evil spirits that drive them deeper into their perversion. (God loves homosexuals but hates their sins.) The perversion of homosexuals then causes the curse of sickness in the form of AIDS to come upon them. AIDS is not incurable, as far as God is concerned, because He can heal any disease. However, a person with AIDS must come to the Lord and be born again. Then he must go through the process for dealing with curses: Repent, renounce the sin, and publicly confess the Lord Jesus Christ. There is no disease for which healing has not been provided in the atonement (Isaiah 53:5; 1 Peter 2:24).

Sins in the following areas make room in a person where demons have a right to live:

Fear, depression, anxiety, loneliness, self-pity, rejection, resentment, hate, rebellion, impatience, pride, unforgiveness, jealousy, envy, covetousness, lust, doubt, greed, and other negative emotions, habits, and thoughts.

Galatians 5:19-21 gives an additional list of such sins that are works of the flesh through which Satan can gain a foothold. Other manifestations of demonic activity in a person's life include suicidal tendencies, some instances of impotency and frigidity, sleepwalking, nailbiting (if compulsive), bedwetting in children, and other habits that are compulsive. Some people are compulsively clean, washing their hands many, many times a day. The late financier and inventor Howard Hughes manifested the demonic symptom of fear of germs to an insane degree.

Demons look for "doors" of sin in our lives through which they can enter and do their evil work. That is why we must repent and obey God, so we can lead pure lives where the devil can find no entry.

Spirits of whoredom or seducing spirits are those who usually gain power over people involved in false religions, cults, and the occult. These are spirits of idolatry, deceiving spirits, and spirits of witchcraft. People afflicted with these may do a lot of "religious" talking, but it does not come from a true spiritual standpoint. Also, demons can inhabit inanimate objects, even houses.

Demons that appear to infest houses — because at some point, they have been allowed in — are called "poltergeists." Most of the time, they are thought to be "ghosts" or "haunts" by people who do not believe in spiritual things or even by Christians who lack knowledge of demonology. These spirits cause weird sights, sounds, and smells. They impersonate dead people. This kind of spirit is also behind all of the UFO sightings and the sightings of "space entities" or beings from another planet that some people "see."

1 Timothy 4:1 warns of the latter times when some shall depart from the faith and give heed to seducing spirits and doctrines of devils. Those "little green men" from outer space that people see really are demons manifesting because of some kind of occult involvement in their lives.

Unclean spirits also may attack the body, not necessarily through sins of the person. This can perhaps happen through generational weaknesses inherited because of the sin of some ancestor that has affected the bodies of his descendants. These inherited diseases include infirmities such as tumors, hayfever, cancers, crippling diseases, arthritis, blindness, ulcers, migraine headaches, asthma and allergies, epilepsy, heart problems, fevers, and other tormenting diseases (Matthew 17:14,15; Mark 3:10,11).

Generational Weaknesses

Sometimes demonic activity and torment are in someone's life, although that person is not guilty of any known sin. This can come about through a "chain of iniquity," which is a curse that comes down on one generation because of the sins of previous generations (Ex. 20:3,5,6; Jer. 32:18,19). On the positive side, people whose ancestors were Godfearing and obedient receive blessings unmerited by themselves. There are "chains of blessings." Timothy is an example, as he inherited his mother's and grandmother's faith (2 Timothy 1:5).

Chains of iniquity can be broken over a person's life by the process of repentance, renouncing them, and then maintaining one's freedom by walking in obedience to the Word of God.

Other curses spoken in the Bible also must be broken in prayer. These are words spoken by someone else over a person or words spoken by that person about himself that do not agree with the Word of God. A curse is the opposite of a blessing. It is an "evil word." The blessings and curses in **Deuteronomy 28** and **Leviticus 26** for God's Old Testament people are the same for us. Yes, our covenant is a <u>better</u> covenant (**Heb. 8:6**), but that does not mean there is no possibility of breaking it. We must choose whom we will serve — the devil or God.

Every contract has clauses that spell out what happens if we keep it and what happens if we break it. Otherwise, it is not a contract but a "deed." The blood covenant of the Old Testament sealed with the blood of animals was a substitute for the <u>real</u> blood sacrifice, Jesus. The New Covenant is better: It is the <u>ratified</u> covenant.

However, there are still penalties for breaking covenant. The choice is ours as to what kind of life we choose: sin with curses as a consequence or obedience with blessings as a result. Demons watch closely for Christians who are not walking in righteousness, or are immature and childish, or are unstable (double-minded, full of fear and doubt) so that he might devour them (1 Peter 5:8).

Curses not only affect people directly but indirectly, just as demons can cause people to stumble (Rev. 2:14). Curses work because <u>there is power in words</u>. Proverbs 12:13,14 says we are snared by our lips. Proverbs 18:20,21 says death and life are in the power of the tongue. James 3 describes in detail the power of the tongue.

The good news is that if we repent of our sins and obey God, we need never to fear curses coming upon us, spoken or otherwise. Deuteronomy 23:4,5 says that God will turn every curse into a blessing for those who <u>love</u> Him. Prayer can break any curse against a Christian. However, we should never send a curse back to the one who spoke it but overcome evil with good (Rom. 12:14,17,21). We must forgive those who curse us and pray for them to come to the knowledge of the truth.

Christ Unlimited — P.O. Box 850 — Dewey, AZ 86327   USA

Luke 6:28 says:

Bless them that curse you, and pray for them which despite-
fully use you.

Christ Unlimited — P.O. Box 850 — Dewey, AZ 86327   USA

Lesson for Section Five

[Author's Note: Please read expository introduction and pages 50-58 of Chapter 3 in <u>Exposing Satan's Devices</u> before beginning this lesson.]

I. Guidelines for Casting Out Demons

   A. Deliverance should be conducted only by _____ Christians.

      1. Casting out demons in others is not risky but requires

        _____.

      2. _____ is the most common device of Satan to keep believers from casting out demons.

      3. Believers should never fear demons because:

      _____.

      Reference:

      Ye are of God, little children, and have overcome them: because greater is he that is in you, than he that is in the world.

                            1 John 4:4

   B. The most important requirement for a Christian involved in casting out demons is _____.

      References: Matthew 17:14-21; Mark 9:17-29

C. Unbelievers should never attempt deliverance. Why?

_____

   1. What happened to the exorcist-sons of Sceva?
      Reference: Acts 19:14-16

_____

   2. Why were they overcome?

_____

II. Methods of Casting Out Demons

   A. Be led by the _____ as to the method.

   B. Should you lay hands on people while casting out devils?

_____

   C. Should you plead the blood of Jesus over people?

_____

_____

   D. Should anyone carry on a conversation with demons during deliverances?

_____

   Reference:

And he healed many that were sick of divers diseases and cast out many devils; and suffered not the devils to <u>speak</u>, because they knew him.

Mark 1:34

   E. Where do demons go when cast out?

Christ Unlimited — P.O. Box 850 — Dewey, AZ 86327   USA

1. _____

2. _____

3. _____

References:

And he besought him much that he would not send them away out of the country.

Mark 5:10

And they besought him that he would not command them to go out into the deep.

Luke 8:31

F. Can demons be destroyed?

_____

G. Is all of Satan's power automatically overcome by Christ's presence within us, or must we do something? _____

_____

Having therefore these promises, dearly beloved, let us cleanse ourselves from all filthiness of the flesh and spirit, perfecting holiness in the fear of God.

2 Corinthians 7:1

Also read Colossians 3:5-14, Ephesians 2:2-10

Christ Unlimited — P.O. Box 850 — Dewey, AZ 86327   USA

H. Deliverance is usually gained by other people's prayers and maintained by staying _____ with the Holy Spirit.

References: Matthew 12:43-45; John 5:14

III. Manifestations and Symptoms of Demonic Oppression

A. Manifestations that can occur when a person is receiving deliverance include:

1. _____   4. _____

2. _____   5. _____

3. _____   6. _____

References: Mark 9:26-28; Luke 8:27,28

And unclean spirits, when they saw him, fell down before him, and cried, saying, Thou art the Son of God.

Mark 3:11

B. Some symptoms of demonic activity are problems that are:

1. _____   4. _____

2. _____   5. _____

3. _____   6. _____

C. The Bible speaks of several kinds of evil spirits that can be behind overpowering sins. Name some of them:

1. _____   3. _____

2. _____   4. _____

5. _____   8. _____

6. _____   9. _____

7. _____   10. _____

D. Some areas in our souls to which Satan attaches unclean spirits, if we continue to embrace these sins, are:

1. _____   5. _____

2. _____   6. _____

3. _____   7. _____

4. _____   8. _____

9. _____   13. _____

10. _____   14. _____

11. _____   15. _____

12. _____   16. _____

Now the works of the flesh are manifest, which are these; Adultery, fornication, uncleanness, lasciviousness, Idolatry, witchcraft, hatred, variance, emulations, wrath, strife, seditions, heresies, Envyings, murders, drunkenness, revellings and such like: of the which I tell you before, as I have also told you in time past, that they which do such things shall not inherit the kingdom of God.

Galatians 5:19-21

E. Unclean spirits that can attack the body are called spirits of infirmity. They include:

1. _____   5. _____

2. _____   6. _____

3. _____   7. _____

4. _____   8. _____

9. _____   11. _____

10. _____   12. _____

For he had healed many; insomuch that they pressed upon him for to touch him, as many as had plagues. And unclean spirits, when they saw him, fell down before him, and cried, saying, Thou art the Son of God.

Mark 3:10,11

When Jesus saw that the people came running together, he rebuked the foul spirit, saying unto him, Thou dumb and deaf spirit, I charge thee, come out of him, and enter no more into him.

Mark 9:25

(Read **Mark 9:17-29** for the complete story.)

F. Spirits that usually influence those involved in false religions, cults, and the occult are called:

_____ spirits and spirits of _____.

1. They are deceiving and witchcraft spirits that manifest
   as _____ spirits.

2. They can _____ the gifts of the Holy
   Spirit.

3. They can manifest in strange, supernatural happenings,
   such as:
   a. _____, _____, _____.
   b. Supernatural _____, such as
      apparitions (ghosts), spirits of dead people,
      and space beings (1 Timothy 4:1).

IV. Concerning Curses (Deuteronomy 28)

A. Evil spirits can torment some people because of a "chain
   of iniquity." What is this?

   _____

   References: Exodus 20:3,5,6; Jeremiah 32:18,19

B. Unmerited blessings also can be received, if our fathers_____
   and_____ with the Lord.
   References: Deuteronomy 30:19,20; 2 Timothy 1:5

C. Can a curse spoken against a Christian by someone operating
   in witchcraft cause that person harm?

   _____

Christ Unlimited — P.O. Box 850 — Dewey, AZ 86327   USA

1. What is a curse? _____

2. What is a blessing? _____
References:

Proverbs 8:6-8 (My mouth shall speak truth.)

Proverbs 12:13,14 (You are snared by your lips.)

Proverbs 18:20,21 (Life and death are in the tongue.)

Christ hath redeemed us from the curse of the law, being made a curse for us: for it is written, Cursed is every one that hangeth on a tree: That the blessing of Abraham might come on the Gentiles through Jesus Christ; that we might receive the promise of the Spirit through faith.

                                        Galatians 3:13,14

D. Satan can use his emissaries against Christians who:

   1. _____ God's way.

   2. _____ and childish.

   3. _____ in their souls.
Reference: 2 Peter 2:14-17

E. Curses can affect people directly and _____,

by causing them to stumble.

Reference: **Revelation 2:14**

F. What can we do to be sure a curse will never come upon us?

_____ and _____ God.

Reference: **Deuteronomy 30:19,20**

G. What can break any curse against a Christian?

_____

H. What should be our reaction against those who have cursed us?

_____

References: **Luke 6:28; Romans 12:14,17,21**

Christ Unlimited — P.O. Box 850 — Dewey, AZ 86327   USA

Overcoming Life Memory Verse

The suggested memory verse for this lesson is:

Ye are of God, little children, and have overcome them:
because greater is he that is in you, than he that is in the world.

1 John 4:4

Christ Unlimited — P.O. Box 850 — Dewey, AZ 86327   USA

Review Outline, Section Five

[**Author's Note**: This outline is from <u>Exposing Satan's Devices</u>, Chapter 3, pages 50-58]

I. Casting Out Demons

  A. Those who should be operating in deliverances are:

    1. People who are not only born again, but Spirit-filled

    2. Christians who walk in faith

  B. Believers are commanded to do so in the Great Commission (Mark 16:15-18).

  C. Methods of Deliverance

    1. Laying on of hands during deliverance

      a. **Lay hands suddenly on no man** (1 Timothy 5:22) refers to ordination, not deliverance.

      b. Demons cannot transfer to us, if we are not in fear.

    2. Casting out demons should be done by listening very carefully to the Holy Spirit to discern what needs to be done.

    3. The blood of Jesus should be pleaded:

      a. As the Holy Spirit leads

        1) Pleading the blood of Jesus will not bring any protection apart from faith in what the blood of Jesus accomplished for us.

2) His blood <u>in itself</u> apart from Him has no "magic" about it and should not be idolized.

4. Do not carry on conversations with demons during deliverances, but command the demons not to speak.

5. Once demons are cast out, the person must:

a. Ask the Holy Spirit to fill the void

b. Work at "crucifying" the flesh area that allowed demons access: temper, greed, lust, or whatever

II. Manifestations During Deliverance and Symptoms of Oppression

A. People being delivered may cry, scream, weep, fall down as dead, wallow on the ground, foam at the mouth, or vomit.

B. There may be <u>no</u> outward manifestation, but they simply have a feeling of relief after deliverance.

C. Symptoms include problems that are unreasonable, abnormal, tormenting, enslaving, addicting, or uncontrollable, such as perverted sex acts, grinding of teeth, talking in one's sleep, bed wetting, hyperactivity, insanity, extremely high or low I.Q., unrelieved grief, strife and contention, phobias and manias, unusual weakness, loss of memory, and other such things that are not ordinary can be symptoms of demons.

D. Infirmities caused by unclean spirits may be fatal diseases, tumors, cancers, crippling afflictions, and extremely painful diseases.

Christ Unlimited — P.O. Box 850 — Dewey, AZ 86327   USA

III. Curses: Inherited and Spoken

A. Inherited curses are consequences of forefathers' actions.

1. Chains of iniquities bring curses upon future generations from the sins of the fathers.

2. Blessings also can be inherited from godly ancestors (2 Timothy 1:5).

3. When we become born again, we have a new Father, God.

   a. A born-again person no longer inherits the curses.

   b. However, the blessings are not automatic.

      1) We must renounce the sins that allow the curse.

      2) We must appropriate by faith the blessings that now are ours (Galatians 3:14,29).

B. Spoken curses

1. Deliberate curses sent forth by those who practice witchcraft

2. Evil (or ungodly) negative words spoken over us by others or by ourselves

3. Curses can affect people directly or indirectly.

C. Curses can be turned to blessings:

1. Through repentance, renouncing, and prayer

2. Through faith in God's Word

3. By overcoming evil with good

Christ Unlimited — P.O. Box 850 — Dewey, AZ 86327   USA

Review Outline Quiz, Section Five

1. Who should cast out demons?

    _____

2. Give the scripture from which we get our Biblical authority
    for casting out demons.

    _____

3. List some possible manifestations of demons during deliverances.

    _____

4. Should we talk to demons to find out their names or
    assignments during deliverance sessions? _____

5. What are curses?

    _____

6. Name one infirmity that may be caused by an unclean spirit.

    _____

7. Are all blessings automatic for Christians? _____

8. How do we get the blessings? _____

    _____

9. Name one type of spoken curses: _____

10. How can curses be turned into blessings? _____

    _____

Exposing Satan's Devices Workbook

Section Six:

"The Christian's Authority Over the Devil"

Christ Unlimited — P.O. Box 850 — Dewey, AZ 86327   USA

Exposing Satan's Devices Workbook
Section Six: "The Christian's Authority Over the Devil"
Expository Introduction

This lesson concludes our examination of the methods and devices used by Satan to deceive people and gain control over them. As we understand how Satan works against people, we can better defeat him and gain the victory. The Bible not only explains the devil's devices, but instructs us in how to overcome him. God has given us various weapons to use in spiritual warfare.

The tactic Satan uses most often against Christians is to bring deception in a "religious" cloak. As we have seen, he will even counterfeit the gifts of the Spirit, and his deceptions usually have threads of truth running through them. Therefore, if we experience any supernatural manifestations, they <u>must</u> line up with the Word of God and the inward witness of the Spirit.

One of the most important things one can get out of this study is that <u>Christians have authority over the devil</u>. Spiritual ignorance is probably the greatest problem among Christians. Lack of knowledge results in defeated lives (Hosea 4:6). Many Christians do not even understand who the enemy is, and consequently, they mistakenly confront people instead of the devil, which produces strife, division, and disunity.

To gain victory over Satan and his kingdom, we must be aware of two things:

1. Spiritual laws and how they operate.

2. Spiritual warfare and how to deal with the devil and his schemes in the realm of the spirit (2 Cor. 10:3,4).

It is useless to reason with someone suffering from demonic oppression. Such afflicted persons cannot understand since they are spiritually blind. Authority must be taken in the situation on a spiritual level. Also, Christians must learn not to be discouraged if they do not receive immediate answers to their prayers. Sometimes it requires a spiritual battle to win our objectives in prayer (Dan. 10:12,13). The moment we begin speaking the Word of God in faith, things _do_ begin to happen in the spirit realm.

As we continue our prayers and battle in faith, it is like providing spiritual ammunition for the angels to work on our behalf. Too often, we give up too soon, cutting off the ammunition supply for the angels of the Lord. If there is difficulty in getting an answer, it may be necessary to find a fellow Christian to pray in agreement with us.

Persevering faith will bring the victory (2 Tim. 4:7). Wherever the devil has a stronghold — health, finances, relationships, or business — we should stand in faith and battle through to victory (1 Tim. 1:18; Joel 2:11). To secure anything in the Lord involves a battle against Satan, who does not want us to have God's provisions.

The first step to getting victory over the devil is to recognize his attacks in our lives.

In the Word of God, we are told how to fight spiritual battles and what weapons are at our disposal. We are to "put on the whole armor of God" (Eph. 6:10,11). We are not to arm ourselves in the flesh, since the battle is a spiritual one.

The battleground is the mind (2 Cor. 10:3-5). We must set our wills to receive only the thoughts that line up with God's will. We need to bring every "alien" thought against God or His Word into captivity. To do that, we must catch the devil in the act of putting wrong thoughts into our minds.

In order to accomplish this, we must know God and His Word well enough to recognize thoughts that accuse God or other people. Satan is "the accuser of the brethren" (Rev. 12:10). So you can be sure that any thoughts are from the enemy that begin with doubt, judgment of others, or accusations. We need to choose against those thoughts, pull them down, and cast them from our minds to get rid of them.

Our thought life is the gateway to our hearts, or our spiritual lives (Prov. 4:23). Temptation begins as carnal or ungodly thoughts are slipped into our minds by a demon.

Christians also have great battles in replacing doctrines and traditions with the Word of God. Many times traditions of men do not line up with God's Word (Matt. 15:3,9). For example, Halloween is a "traditional" holiday that is openly satanic. We must not be involved with celebrating this day simply because it is a tradition in our nation.

Resisting the devil takes effort. He may not flee the very first time we order him to do so. Usually, demons will not cease harassing us, if we are passive and not actively warring against them.

Jesus gained his victory over Satan by rebuking him. He even rebuked the devil, when he influenced Peter (**Mark 8:31-33**). On the positive side, Jesus also recognized the influence of the Holy Spirit in Peter's life (**Matt. 16:16,17**). Jesus rebuked the devil, but loved Peter. He told Peter that He had prayed for him (**Luke 22:31,32**).

Retaliation is not the way to overcome strife and the devil. As we learned in the last lesson, Jesus told us to overcome evil with good (**Romans 12:17-21; Galatians 5:14,15**).

Spiritual Armor and Weapons

We are told in **Ephesians 6** to put on the armor of God to do battle with the devil. The first piece of armor is truth (**Eph. 6:14**). The Holy Spirit is the Spirit of Truth. According to **1 Peter 1:13**, having our "loins girt with truth" is talking about the mind. We cannot fill our minds with secular concepts, ideas, and facts from hours of television, worldly reading, and movies, yet still expect to walk in God's light.

Allowing the Holy Spirit full authority over the mind protects the whole person. You cannot sin without thinking about it first. The "loins" are the private, procreative parts of man and woman. So the "loins" of the mind are the imaginative faculties through which creativity comes into our lives. Our minds "give birth" to our actions.

Christ Unlimited — P.O. Box 850 — Dewey, AZ 86327   USA

Guarding our minds includes thinking godly thoughts concerning our brethren, rather than critical thoughts. By reading God's Word, loving and obeying Jesus with our whole minds and hearts, and fellowshipping with the Holy Spirit daily, we can gird up our loins with truth.

The second piece of a Christian's armor is <u>the breastplate of righteousness</u> (**Eph. 6:14**). One tactic of the devil is to attempt to bring condemnation on Christians by whispering into their minds that they cannot ask anything of God because of a certain sin or error they have committed in the past. Demons attempt to keep Christians from running <u>to</u> God when they fail Him. Our defense against condemnation and the wrong kind of fear (a tormenting fear) of God is the breastplate of righteousness.

We can voice to the devil these words, "Devil, my God has forgiven me of the sins I have confessed to Him, so according to His Word in **1 John 1:9**, I am not only forgiven but cleansed from unrighteousness."

It is not <u>our</u> righteousness that has gained the victory, but it is Jesus' righteousness that was imputed to us when we were born again (**2 Corinthians 5:19**).

His righteousness was not <u>imparted</u> (actually made part of us) any more than our sins actually were <u>imparted</u> to Him. His righteousness was <u>imputed</u> (credited to our account) and our sins were credited to His account (imputed), but they never became part of Him. He never sinned.

His righteousness makes it possible for us to approach God and live. From the time we become born again, the Holy Spirit works in our lives to bring us into conformity with that righteousness. It is something like a white robe that covers all of our blemishes, stains, and defects from the sight of God. And the Holy Spirit works with us under the robe to clean us up. That is called sanctification or coming into holiness.

Righteousness means "to be in right-standing" with God, and through Jesus we are. However, repenting of sin, renouncing it, and asking the Holy Spirit to cleanse us causes us to conform in that area to the righteousness of Jesus. We should not walk under condemnation (**Rom. 8:1**). When God forgives you, He forgets that sin. Neither you nor the devil should bring it up again. It is as though it never happened, as far as God's remembrance is concerned (**Ps. 103:12; Hebrews 8:12**).

The third piece of armor is the gospel of peace (**Eph. 6:15**). We are to have our feet "shod" with the gospel of peace. That means we are to take that gospel of peace to others, and we are to be peacemakers (**Matt. 5:9; Eph. 4:3**). Because of Jesus, we are at peace with God (**Romans 5:1**).

Because of Jesus, we have been reconciled to God (**2 Cor. 5:19**). God never needed to be reconciled to mankind, because He never moved from His position of love toward us. However, Scripture says mankind had to be reconciled to God. We are the ones who walked away from Him.

Christ Unlimited — P.O. Box 850 — Dewey, AZ 86327   USA

The <u>shield of faith</u> (Eph. 6:16) is the fourth piece of armor. Christians should only be moved by faith, not by fear, any selfish motive, or by circumstances. If we do anything that does not involve an act of faith toward God, that thing is sin (Romans 14:23).

The fifth piece of armor is <u>the helmet of salvation</u> (Eph. 6:17). This "helmet" is designed to protect not only our minds but all of us (Phil. 4:7,8). This "helmet" is the symbol of the blood covenant, because salvation is the covenant relationship we have with God through Jesus. It represents the blood that was placed on the door posts of the Israelites in Egypt to protect them from the death angel. This "Passover" was a shadow or a type of the New Covenant.

The sixth piece of the armor of God is <u>the sword of the Spirit</u>, which is the Word of God (Eph. 6:17). This is an offensive weapon rather than a defensive piece of armor. The Word of God is the weapon that drives off the enemy.

God is looking for aggressive believers who will use His Word to take territory back from the devil for the Kingdom of God. We should not be running from the devil. He should be running from us. We are to take the offensive. Jesus overcame the devil by speaking the Word of God to him (Matt. 4:4), and so can we. We are conquerors through Jesus (Romans 8:11, 8:37; John 15:7).

Prayer Goes With Our Armor

After putting on our armor, we are given our "marching orders" of prayer (Eph. 6:18). Prayer is the necessary key for overcoming the devil. Note that all <u>kinds</u> of prayer are mentioned in **Ephesians 6:18**: praying in the natural and praying in the Spirit (with tongues — 1 Corinthians 14:2).

Warring in the Spirit sometimes can be loud and noisy as we must forcefully and loudly command the devil to depart and loose his hold on those things he has been binding. War is not quiet, therefore we should use wisdom regarding who is exposed to our warring in the Spirit. We are also to watch and persevere, which means to be persistent in prayer, and also to maintain a disciplined prayer life.

Having put on the whole armor of light, we are able to overcome all darkness (**Romans 13:12**).

The war actually is taking place in two dimensions: the seen and the unseen, the natural and the supernatural. When we gain victory in the unseen, it then manifests in the seen. Also, within the supernatural dimension are two realms: God's and the devil's. The lower regions are relegated to Satan, his demons, fallen angels, and lost souls of mankind. We must understand the existence of the supernatural, which we sometimes call "the spiritual world."

There are only two real kingdoms on earth: the Kingdom of Light, which is God's, and the Kingdom of Darkness, over which Satan rules. And, although defeated, Satan is still ruling over his kingdom on earth. Both he and his troops must bow their knees and give up the territory they are claiming as we exercise authority over them. If we have been losing our battles in the natural realm and the devil has been robbing from us, then we need to do warfare in the supernatural realm with our weapons of warfare. We are assured of victory, because the devil is no match for the believer who knows his authority in Jesus (**2 Corinthians 10:3,4**).

Lesson for Section Six

[Author's Note: This lesson is based on Chapter 4 of Exposing Satan's Devices and on the preceding expository introduction to this section. Please read both before answering the questions.]

I. Warfare Against the Devil

A. What is the greatest problem among Christians today, which results in defeated lives and missing God?

_____

Reference: Hosea 4:6

B. To gain victory over Satan and his kingdom, we must be aware of _____ and _____ _____.

Reference: 2 Corinthians 10:3,4

C. Why do we have authority over Satan, and how can we use it?

_____

_____

_____

References: Luke 10:18,19,11:20; 1 John 3:8

D. We should not be discouraged if we do not get immediate answers to our prayers. Spiritual _____ may be required before we can win our prayer objectives.

Then said he unto me, Fear not, Daniel: for from the first day that thou didst set thine heart to understand, and to chasten thyself before thy God, thy words were heard, and I am come for thy words. But the prince of the kingdom of Persia withstood me one and twenty days: but, lo, Michael, one of the chief princes, came to help me; and I remained there with the kings of Persia.

Daniel 10:12,13

E. Today, we have been challenged to stand up as part of the _____ of _____ and fight the same kind of spiritual battle that Daniel and Paul fought.

This charge I commit unto thee, son Timothy, according to the prophecies which went before on thee, that thou by them mightest war a good warfare.

I have fought a good fight, I have finished my course, I have kept the faith.

1 Timothy 1:18; 2 Timothy 4:7

And the Lord shall utter his voice before his army: for his camp is very great: for he is strong that executeth his word: for the day of the Lord is great and very terrible; who can abide it?

Joel 2:11

Christ Unlimited — P.O. Box 850 — Dewey, AZ 86327   USA

II. Concerning Spiritual Warfare

A. How do Christians fight battles?

_____

> Finally, my brethren, be strong in the Lord, and in the power of his might. Put on the whole armour of God, that ye may be able to stand against the wiles of the devil.
>
> Ephesians 6:10,11

B. Where is the main battleground?

_____

> For though we walk in the flesh, we do not war after the flesh: (For the weapons of our warfare are not carnal, but mighty through God to the pulling down of strong holds;) Casting down imaginations, and every high thing that exalteth itself against the knowledge of God, and bringing into captivity every thought to the obedience of Christ.
>
> 2 Corinthians 10:3-5

1. We must realize our warfare is not in the flesh, but in the _____ _____.

2. We must bring every alien thought against _____ _____ into captivity.

3. The first step to getting victory over the devil is to _____ him.

4. The thought life must be guarded, as it is the gateway
   to the life of the _____.
   Reference: **Proverbs 4:23**

5. Temptation is defined as a carnal or evil _____
   presented to one's mind by the devil.
   Reference: **Romans 12:2**

C. We must recognize and renounce the _____
   of _____ and replace them with the Word of God
   when they do not line up with Scripture.
   Reference: **Matthew 15:3-9**

D. To stand against the wiles of the devil, we must
   _____ him.
   References: **James 4:7; Ephesians 6:12**

1. We must remember our battle is with _____
   and not with people.

2. Jesus _____ Satan, when speaking to Peter
   (**Mark 8:31-33**).

3. Jesus also recognized the influence of the_____
   _____ in Peter's life (**Matthew 16:16,17**).

4. How did Jesus handle the problem of the enemy coming
   through his beloved disciple, Peter?

   _____

And the Lord said, Simon, Simon, behold, Satan hath desired to have you, that he may sift you as wheat: But I have prayed for thee, that thy faith fail not: and when thou art converted, strengthen thy brethren.

Luke 22:31,32

5. Retaliation is not the way to overcome _____ and the devil.

References: Romans 12:17-21; Galatians 5:14,15

III. The Christian's Weapons and Warfare

A. The Armor of God

1. The Belt of Truth (Ephesians 6:14)

a. Define "loins girt with truth" (Romans 12:2).

_____

b. How do we gird our loins with truth? (Ephesians 4:23)

_____

Reference: 1 Peter 1:13

2. The Breastplate of Righteousness (Ephesians 6:14)

a. What is the definition of the word, <u>righteousness</u>? The Greek word translated "righteousness" in the <u>King James Version of the Holy Bible</u> means "to be just," or to be in:

_____

b. Do we have any righteousness of our own? _____

Christ Unlimited — P.O. Box 850 — Dewey, AZ 86327   USA

...There is none righteous, no, not one.

Romans 3:10

But we are all as an unclean thing, and all our righteousnesses are as filthy rags ...

Isaiah 64:6

c. When we are born again, we receive the <u>righteousness</u> of _____ through Jesus.

Reference: 2 Corinthians 5:19-21

1) We should not allow the devil's lies to put

_____ on us.

2) We should know that we are _____ through Jesus.

There is therefore now no condemnation to them which are in Christ Jesus, who walk not after the flesh, but after the Spirit.

Romans 8:1

3. The next piece of armor is to have our feet shod with the _____ (Ephesians 6:15).

a. The message of the gospel of peace is: Because of Jesus, mankind can now have _____ with God.

Christ Unlimited — P.O. Box 850 — Dewey, AZ 86327   USA

Therefore being justified by <u>faith</u>, we have <u>peace</u> with God through our Lord Jesus Christ.

Romans 5:1

b. Secondly, we are to be _____.

Endeavouring to keep the unity of the Spirit in the bond of peace.

Ephesians 4:3

Blessed are the peacemakers: for they shall be called the children of God.

Matthew 5:9

4. The fourth piece of armor is _____ (Ephesians 6:16).
   a. If we are moved by fear, circumstances, selfishness or any other like motive, it is not _____.
   b. If we do anything that is not an act of faith toward God, it is _____ _____.

...For whatsoever is not of faith is sin.

Romans 14:23

5. The Helmet of Salvation is the fifth piece of armor (Ephesians 6:17).
   a. We must guard our minds by _____ the right thoughts (Philippians 4:7,8).

b. The _____ is the area of the mind that must

be controlled.

Reference: 2 Corinthians 10:5

6. The last "weapon" mentioned in Ephesians 6:17 is:

_____.

a. This is an _____ weapon.

b. We are to be conquerors and _____ in Jesus.

For whatsoever is born of God overcometh the world: and this is the victory that overcometh the world, even our faith. Who is he that overcometh the world, but he that believeth that Jesus is the Son of God?

1 John 5:4,5

Nay, in all these things we are more than conquerors through him that loved us.

Romans 8:37

If ye abide in me, and my words abide in you, ye shall ask what ye will, and it shall be done unto you.

John 15:7

c. Jesus is our example in fighting the devil, as He is

in all other things. He overcame Satan by _____

Christ Unlimited — P.O. Box 850 — Dewey, AZ 86327   USA

_____ the Word of God to him.

   Reference: Matthew 4:4

B. Marching orders follow putting on the _____

   _____ of _____ (Ephesians 6:13).

   1. Prayer is_____ necessary for overcoming

      the devil (Ephesians 6:18).

      a. Two kinds of prayer in 1 Corinthians 14:15 are:

         1) _____

         2) _____

      b. Praying in the Spirit means "praying in _____."

         Reference: 1 Corinthians 14:2

   2. Warring in the Spirit sometimes can be _____.

      a. We should use _____ concerning who hears us

         doing warfare in the Spirit, because we are speaking to

         the devil, and men will not understand.

      b. We are to watch and persevere, which is to be

         _____ in prayer (Ephesians 6:18).

      c. We also are to maintain a _____ prayer life

         (1 Thessalonians 5:17).

3. Having put on our armor of _____, we shall be able to overcome all darkness.

> The night is far spent, the day is at hand: let us therefore cast off the works of darkness, and let us put on the armour of light.
>
> Romans 13:12

To conclude this lesson, please read Ephesians 1:17-23 as a prayer. God bless each student who has taken this course and those who continue to study the Word of God!

Christ Unlimited — P.O. Box 850 — Dewey, AZ 86327   USA

Overcoming Life Memory Verse

The suggested memory verses for this section are:

Put on the whole armour of God, that ye may be able to stand against the wiles of the devil. For we wrestle not against flesh and blood, but against principalities, against powers, against the rulers of the darkness of this world, against spiritual wickedness in high places.

Ephesians 6:11,12

Review Outline, Section Six

[**Author's Note:** This outline is taken from pp. 59-73 of <u>Exposing Satan's Devices</u>.]

I. War Between the Kingdoms

   A. There are two dimensions, two realms of the spiritual world, and two kingdoms on earth:

   1. Natural and supernatural

   2. Heaven and Hell

   3. Kingdom of Light and Kingdom of Darkness

   B. These two kingdoms are at war in the earth.

   1. The Kingdom of Light has these inhabitants:

      a. The Holy Spirit, who directs warfare on earth under instructions from Jesus, the Head of the Church, and the Father God

      b. Angels and other heavenly beings

      c. Christians

         1) Not all Christians involve themselves in this warfare; therefore, many live defeated lives.

         2) Christians enlist in God's army when they are born again, but some are "slackers" and some "deserters."

   2. The Kingdom of Darkness has these inhabitants:

      a. Satan

      b. Demons

      c. Fallen angels

d. Men and women who allow demons to use them to put forward the plans of the enemy of God

II. Weapons of Warfare: The Armor of God
(Ephesians 6:10-18)

A. Defensive weapons

1. The helmet of salvation, which gives:

   a. Security concerning eternity through becoming born again

   b. Protects our thought lives from the intrusion of Satan's temptations by walking in the Holy Spirit

2. The belt of truth with which we "gird up" our "loins"

   a. The Holy Spirit is the Spirit of Truth.

   b. He protects the "loins" of the mind: imagination, also reason, memory, and thought life.

      1) Like everything else Jesus provided for mankind on the cross, the Spirit of truth does not come automatically.

         a) The mind must be given to the Holy Spirit as much as the body placed on the altar for service.

         b) We receive His protection and the renewing of our minds by faith.

      2) The mind is the battleground of spiritual warfare.

3. The breastplate of righteousness

    a. Christ's righteousness covers our hearts.

    b. "Self"-righteousness is a counterfeit breastplate and stems from religious pride (**Romans 3:10; Isaiah 64:6**).

4. Sandals of the Gospel of peace

    a. This means sharing Jesus with others, the ministry of reconciliation (**Romans 5:1; 2 Corinthians 5:18**).

    b. We also should be peacemakers (**Matthew 5:9**).

    c. We also walk in His peace in our personal lives.

5. The shield of faith

    a. This means totally trusting in Jesus.

    b. The Word of God is to be part of us, the fruit of faith.

    c. Any act not done in faith is sin (**Romans 14:23**).

B. Offensive weapons

1. The sword of the Spirit

    a. Make a spirited offense against the devil using the Word of God, as Jesus did (**Matthew 4:1-11**).

    b. Jesus <u>is</u> the Living Word (**John 1:1**).

    c. Through Him and the written Word, we can be more than conquerors.

2. Prayer (in one's native language and in tongues)

    a. Prayer in tongues speaks directly to God.

    b. Prayer in tongues overcomes plans of the enemy.

3. Other offensive weapons:

    a. Fasting

    b. Warring in the Spirit by confessing the Word of God

    c. The authority of Jesus which we exercise by His name

    d. Gifts of the Spirit, given to the Church, which the Spirit operates through those yielded to Him (1 Corinthians 12)

C. Marching orders given for Christians are:

1. Use our weapons!

2. Pray continually with all kinds of prayer.

3. Resist the devil.

    a. In thought (1 Peter 1:13)

    b. In Word (Luke 4:1-4)

    c. In Deed (James 1:22)

4. We are to make ourselves available for the Holy Spirit to exercise His gifts to the Body of Christ through us.

5. We are to fast to break the enemy's power over certain areas, circumstances, and people (Matthew 6:17,18).

6. We are to study the Word in order to be able to use it, not simply to "claim" promises, but also to resist and defeat the enemy.

Christ Unlimited — P.O. Box 850 — Dewey, AZ 86327   USA

Review Outline Quiz, Section Six

1. How many pieces are there to the armor of God? _____

2. List the various pieces of the armor of God.

    a. _____

    b. _____

    c. _____

    d. _____

    e. _____

    f. _____

3. List three scriptures that show we have power over the devil.

    _____, _____, and _____

4. Which are the defensive parts of the armor of God?

    _____

5. What is the offensive part of the armor? _____

    _____ of the _____

6. List some other offensive weapons God has provided for us to use against the devil.

   a. _____   c. _____

   b. _____   d. _____

7. Who are the Christian's real enemies?

   _____

8. What are the two realms of the spiritual world?

   _____ and _____

9. Before resisting the enemy, what are we told in Scripture to do? Reference: James 4:7

   _____

10. What types of prayer are helpful in our battles of spiritual warfare?

    a. _____

    b. _____

List of Common Cultic or Occultic Snares

For those who have completed this study on <u>Exposing Satan's Devices</u>, we have provided a checklist of the most common cultic or occult snares into which people fall in our day. Please prayerfully ask the Holy Spirit to reveal any area that may have opened a door or doors to Satan in the past. Then, repent of that involvement and renounce it in the name of Jesus in order to be free of any past bondage.

The person who does this from a genuine commitment to God and in faith will experience a very real freedom from any satanic bondage that may have been in his life.

Check the ones in which you personally have been involved, then pray about those. Participation in any way, even "just for fun," can open doors to demonic influence.

I. False Sources of Guidance or Information
    A. Astrology
        _____ 1. Zodiac charts or sign information (Life readings)
        _____ 2. Newspaper astrology columns
        _____ 3. Magazines or books about astrology
        _____ 4. Almanacs

    B. Foretelling the future
        _____ 1. Fortune tellers
        _____ 2. Palm readers
        _____ 3. Readers of tea leaves, and so forth
        _____ 4. The "I Ching" or other Oriental systems
        _____ 5. Crystal ball "seeing"
        _____ 6. Tarot or other card readings
        _____ 7. Fortune cookies, weight-machine fortunes,
               and so forth
        _____ 8. Other practices

    C. _____ Handwriting analysis (Graphology)

    D. Communicating with the dead:
        _____ 1. Seances
        _____ 2. Ouija boards
        _____ 3. Pendulums
            (Also could be under "foretelling the future.")

II. New Age or Psychic Interests
    A. _____ Hypnosis (even medical or dental)
    B. Other health-related areas of participation:

Christ Unlimited — P.O. Box 850 — Dewey, AZ 86327   USA

_____ 1. Acupuncture or acupressure
_____ 2. Biofeedback machines, dots, etc.
_____ 3. Meditation to relieve pain (Many pain clinics use this.)
_____ 4. White magic (removing warts, etc.)
_____ 5. Psychic healing or surgery
_____ 6. Tattoos
_____ 7. Chiropractic treatments (Has roots in Eastern Religion
      & founder Daniel David Palmer was involved in spiritism)

C. Supernatural exercises:
_____ 1. Telepathy
_____ 2. Telekinesis (moving objects with the mind)
_____ 3. Levitation (The body or objects move through the air unaided
      by natural means.)
_____4. Fire Walking
D. Trance-related experiences:
_____ 1. Past life "readings" or experiences
_____ 2. Out-of-body experiences (astral projection)
_____ 3. Trances used to harass others or obtain information about them
      ("Putting on someone else's head")

E. _____ Water-dowsing, or using divining rods to find water or minerals
      etc., also called "water-witching"

F. Witchcraft:
_____ 1. Voodoo or other "spells"
_____ 2. Supernatural magic of any kind
_____ 3. Hexes placed on other people
_____ 4. Making or wearing good luck charms
_____ 5. Wearing fetishes for healing purposes

G. Mind or body programs, or systems of control:
_____ 1. Mind control courses
_____ 2. Yoga
_____ 3. Karate, or other martial arts
_____ 4. Transcendental meditation

H. Spiritualistic/Psychic Religions:
_____ 1. Spiritualist churches
_____ 2. Scientology
_____ 3. Rosicrucianism

I. New Age Music:

_____ 1. Much "nature-related" music

_____ 2. Meditation and subliminal tapes for healing
     or control of bad habits or other reasons

J. _____ Environmental groups rooted in pantheism
(Extremists with great emphasis on "save the animals" but they are totally committed <u>to</u> abortion. They worship the creation more than the Creator (**Romans 1:25**). As Christians, we are to be good stewards over the earth and its animals, but animal life is not equal to human life.)

K. _____ Metaphysics (books, studies, etc.)

III. False Religions and Cults

A. False religions:

_____ 1. Islam (Moslems, or Muslims)

_____ 2. Hinduism

_____ 3. Buddhism

_____ 4. Oriental ancestor worship

_____ 5. Hari Krishna

_____ 6. Bahaism

_____ 7. Native American ancestral religions

_____ 8. Church of Sun Myung Moon (Moonies)

_____ 9. Others, such as animism

B. Cults (contains some Christian truths, but distorted):

_____ 1. The Church of Jesus Christ of the Latter Day Saints
     (Mormonism)

_____ 2. Jehovah's Witnesses

_____ 3. The Way

_____ 4. The Children of God and similar cults, such as the
     Branch Davidians

_____ 5. Christian Science

_____ 6. Science of Mind Church

_____ 7. Swedenborgianism

_____ 8. Unitarian

_____ 9. Unity School of Christianity

_____ 10. Spiritual Frontiers Fellowship (Edgar Cayce)

_____ 11. Universalism

_____ 12. Any other cults

C. _____ Tourist visits to temples or false religion/cultic headquarters_____
(Entering these places can open a door for demonic oppression unless sent

Christ Unlimited — P.O. Box 850 — Dewey, AZ 86327   USA

there on a mission for the Lord. These include places such as Mormon temples, the Islam Dome of the Rock or other mosques in Israel, Native American "pow-wows" or other dances or ceremonies, temples in Japan, China, Korea. Tourist visits to pagan sites, such as in Mexico and South America also can be dangerous.)

IV. Occult Books, Films, or Games
   A. Books based on:
      _____ 1. Horror or ghosts
      _____ 2. Reincarnation
      _____ 3. Exorcism that is not Christian
      _____ 4. Psychic subjects
      _____ 5. Fairy tales and fantasy
      _____ 6. Science fiction
      _____ 7. UFOs

   B. Films:
      _____ 1. Any of the above subjects
      _____ 2. Television series, such as "Kung Fu," "I Dream of Jeannie," and many so-called "children's programs" and cartoons that have witchcraft and supernatural heroes or subjects in them.
      _____ 3. Watching soap operas

   C. Games:
      _____ 1. Dungeons and Dragons
      _____ 2. Many video or computer games such as "Doom"
      _____ 3. Even if the subject matter seems okay, if playing these in arcades or at home has become compulsive, a satanic influence may be at work.

   D. Objects:
      _____ 1. Occult or cultic decorator items, such as evil masks, idols, statues, etc.
      _____ 2. Jewelry that represents false religions, or is made of occult symbols
      _____ 3. Posters or pictures that represent evil, satanic groups, or satanic objects
      _____ 4. Rugs, baskets, or household items that have curses attached to them

V. Direct Satanic Activities
      _____ A. Satanist religion
      _____ B. Mediumistic activity

_____ C. Sacrificing of animals
_____ D. Sorcery

VI. Participation in Secret Societies
 A. The Order of Freemasonry
  _____ 1. Masons of any rites or degrees
  _____ 2. Eastern Star
  _____ 3. Demolay
 B. _____ Fraternities or sororities

VII. Opening the Body to Satanic Influence
 (This can be as dangerous as opening the mind to the things listed above.)
 A. Food or beverage-oriented traps of Satan:
  _____ 1. Making food a substitute for emotional or physical satisfaction
   _____ a. Lust for food
   _____ b. Gluttony
   _____ c. Caffeine, sugar, food or drink addictions
  _____ 2. Substance abuse
   (Alcohol, chemicals, marijuana, etc.)
  _____ 3. Nicotine addiction
  _____ 4. Making health foods a "god" (We are to eat healthy food, and we should be wise in our food choices but avoid the extreme of having everything revolve around eating.)
  _____ 5. Other dependencies, such as exercising to the extreme

 B. Sex-oriented traps:
  _____ 1. Adultery
  _____ 2. Compulsive masturbation
  _____ 3. Child molesting
  _____ 4. Rape
  _____ 5. Homosexuality or lesbianism
  _____ 6. Oral sex
  _____ 7. Sex fantasies
  _____ 8. Incest
  _____ 9. Bestiality
  _____ 10. Pornography (books, movies, or other forms)

VIII. Questions To Reveal Problem Areas:
 _____ A. Have you ever denied the divinity, virgin birth, or resurrection of Christ?
 _____ B. Have you ever made a "blood pact"?
 _____ C. Have you ever been subject to compulsive habits? (Daydreaming, gossiping, lying, stealing, cursing, biting fingernails, or similar things)

Christ Unlimited — P.O. Box 850 — Dewey, AZ 86327 USA

_____ D. Have you been subject to frequently occurring
       emotions? (Rejection, depression, anger, fear hate, etc.)
_____ E. Have you ever had a death wish, for yourself, for
       anyone else, or been tormented with suicidal thoughts?
_____ F. Write in here anything else the Holy Spirit brings
       to your mind. _____

       _____

       _____

Christ Unlimited — P.O. Box 850 — Dewey, AZ 86327   USA

Bibliography

Cults, False Religions:

Adair, James R.; Miller, Ted. We Found Our Way Out (Grand Rapids: Baker Book House, 1964).

Basham, Don. Deliver Us From Evil (Grand Rapids: Chosen Books, 1972).

Cowan, Marvin W. Mormon Claims Answered (1975, 1982).

DeLoach, Charles F. The Armstrong Error (Plainfield: Logos Books, 1971).

Fraser, Gordon H. Is Mormonism Christian?" (Chicago: Moody Bible Institute, 1957, 1965).

Freeman, Hobart E. Angels of Light and Every Wind of Doctrine (Plainfield: Logos International, 1969; Warsaw: Faith Ministries, 1974). [Note: Freeman fell into error in the later years of his life through extremism on healing; however, these books are very good on cults and New Age subjects.]

Martin, Walter R. Kingdom of the Cults (1965, 1985); Jehovah's Witnesses (Minneapolis: Bethany House Publishers, 1957, 1971).

Reed, David. Jehovah's Witnesses (Grand Rapids: Baker Book House,1990).

Deliverance and Spiritual Warfare:

Basham, Don; Prince, Derek. The Unseen War (New Wine Library).

Gasson, Raphael. The Challenging Counterfeit (Plainfield: Logos International, 1969).

Gurnall, William. The Christian in Complete Armour (Carlisle: Banner of Truth Trust, 1986, abridged and reprinted from 1655, 1864 editions).

Hagin, Kenneth E. Satan, Demons, and Demon Possession Series (Tulsa: Rhema Bible Church, 1983). Also The Authority of the Believer.

Hammond, Frank and Ida Mae. Kingdom Living for the Family and Pigs in the Parlor (Kirkwood: Impact Books).

Jacobs, Cindy. The Gates of the Enemy (Tarrytown: Chosen Books, 1991).

Johnson, George; Tanner, Don. The Bible and the Bermuda Triangle (Plainfield: Logos International, 1976).

Mumford, Bob. Take Another Look at Guidance (Altamonte: Creation
   House, 1991).

Penn-Lewis, Jessie. War on the Saints, unabridged. (New York: Thomas E. Lowe Ltd., 1973, 1988).

Stewart, Ken. No Evil Shall Befall Thee (Tulsa: Harrison House, 1991).

Whyte, H. A. Maxwell. Dominion Over Demons (Monroeville: Banner Publishing, 1973).

New Age and Related Subjects:

Allnutt, Frank. Unlocking the Mystery of the Force (Evergreen: Allnutt Publishers, 1983).

Bambridge, A. D. Acupuncture Investigated, Homeopathy Investigated
   (Kent, England: Diasozo Trust, 1989).

Bayly, James. What About Horoscopes? (Elgin: David C. Cook Pub. Co., 1970).

Folz, Joe. Psychic Healers of the Philippines (Plainfield: Logos International, 1981).

Greenwald, Gary L. Seductions Exposed (Santa Ana: Eagle's Nest Publications, 1989).

Michaelsen, Johanna. The Beautiful Side of Evil (Eugene: Harvest House Publishers, 1982).

Marrs, Texe. Dark Secrets of the New Age (Westchester: Crossway Books, 1987.)

Phillips, Phil. Turmoil in the Toybox (Lancaster: Starburst Publishers, 1986).

What You Need to Know About
Christ Unlimited Ministries

Purpose and Vision

Go ye therefore, and teach all nations, baptizing them in the name of the Father, and of the Son, and of the Holy Ghost: Teaching them to observe all things whatsoever I have commanded you: and, lo, I am with you always, even unto the end of the world. Amen.

Matthew 28:19, 20

CHRIST UNLIMITED is not "another denomination," sect, or just a separate group. It is an arm of the Body of Christ — the Church of Jesus Christ, which has been called to strengthen the Body at large. We also believe we have been called to help establish the Kingdom of God in the earth.

CHRIST UNLIMITED is open to help and work with all Bible-believing Christians regardless of their church or denominational affiliations and committed to helping wherever possible in evangelistic and teaching outreaches.

CHRIST UNLIMITED believes that time is running out and the Gospel has not been preached to every creature. Many nations have not heard the Gospel, and in many places, doors for evangelism are closing. We believe it is time all Christians cooperated with the Lord in breaking down denominational walls for a united front line against the kingdom of darkness and in setting up the Kingdom of the Lord Jesus Christ by the power of the Holy Spirit.

CHRIST UNLIMITED provides such tools as to enable the saints of God to establish the Kingdom of God in the earth. We encourage groups of prayer warriors who will pray, fast, and intercede for the nations. This, we believe, is weapon number one. We teach believers how to overcome through spiritual warfare and through knowing how to use their authority in Christ Jesus through the Word and the power of the Holy Spirit.

Christians need to know how to bring down the forces of darkness in their own lives and in the lives of those to whom they minister. We provide such tools as Bibles, literature, **CHRIST UNLIMITED** books, and downloadable audio and video. We promote the Gospel going forth via any means of communication, including radio and video, the INTERNET, and literature. We promote teaching seminars, Bible schools, and correspondence courses, all aimed at winning souls to Christ and building the Body of Christ into maturity.

Bud and Betty Miller serve the Lord together as founders of the multi-vision ministry outreach, **CHRIST UNLIMITED**. The outreaches of this ministry have stemmed from a tremendous desire to see the Word of God taught in its balanced entirety. The Millers are firm believers in prayer and, through prayer, have seen many released from the bondages of fear, failure, and defeat.

Christ Unlimited — P.O. Box 850 — Dewey, AZ 86327 USA

The Millers have a world-wide vision for spreading the full-gospel message and teaching God's Word. Bud not only preaches and pastors a church, but is director of **CHRIST UNLIMITED PUBLISHING**, an outreach dedicated to publishing God's Word in many languages. His experience, openness to the Holy Spirit, and down-to-earth expression of God's love have blessed many. God has endowed Betty with a rare gift of teaching that makes her a practical and effective "handmaiden of the Lord." Both Bud and Betty have hearts turned toward evangelism and missions, desiring to tell everyone of God's wonderful love. Their anointed teaching comes across with simplicity and in the power of the Holy Spirit.

The outreaches of **CHRIST UNLIMITED** are in obedience to the words of our Lord in **Mark 16:15: Go ye into all the world and preach the gospel to every creature.** This mandate from the Lord presents a challenge to our generation as an estimated 25 percent of the world's population still have not heard the Good News of Jesus Christ.[1]

CHRIST UNLIMITED MINISTRIES also is dedicated to teaching God's Word. **Hosea 4:6** says: **My people are destroyed for lack of knowledge.** Many Christians are leading defeated lives simply because they do not know God's Word in its fullest.

CHRIST UNLIMITED MINISTRIES has provided literature for those who desire to know God's Word in a greater way. The main thrust of the teaching and literature is directed at "How to be an overcomer." In the endtimes, we must be prepared to overcome the onslaughts of Satan. Many Christians are suffering needlessly, because they do not know how to overcome sin, sickness, depression, divorce, fear, and financial failure. **CHRIST UNLIMITED MINISTRIES** provides answers for troubled families as well as trains workers for service.

DOCTRINAL STATEMENT

> Jesus answered them, and said, My doctrine is not mine, but his that sent me. If any man will do his will, he shall know of the doctrine, whether it be of God, or whether I speak of myself.
> John 7:16,17

Inspiration of Scriptures: We believe that the Holy Bible is the written Word of the Living God. We believe it was inspired by the Holy Spirit and recorded by holy men of old. It is infallible in content and a perfect treasure of heavenly instruction which is truth without any mixture of error. The Bible reveals the principles by which God will judge us and reveals His great plan of salvation. It will remain eternally. We believe the Bible is the true center of Christian union and the supreme standard by which all human conduct, creeds, and opinions should be tried. Therefore, we believe this Word should go into all the world and should be given first place in every believer's life (2 Tim. 3:16; Heb. 4:12; 1 Pet. 1:23-25; and 2 Pet. 1:19-21).

<u>God:</u> We believe in one God revealed in three persons: the Father, the Son, and the Holy Ghost . . . making up the blessed Trinity (Matt. 3:16,17; 1 John 5:6,7).

<u>Man:</u> We believe that man, in his natural state, is a sinner —lost, undone, without hope, and without God (Rom. 3:19-23; Gal. 3:22; Eph. 2:1,2,12).

<u>Salvation:</u> We believe the terms of salvation are repentance toward God for sin and a personal, heartfelt faith in the Lord Jesus Christ. This will result in a new birth. Salvation is possible only through God's grace, not by our works. Works are simply the <u>fruit</u> of salvation (Acts 3:19,20; Rom. 4:1-5, 5:1; Eph. 2:8-10).

<u>Body of Christ:</u> We believe the Body of Christ is made up of all who have been born again regardless of denominational differences. We believe in the spirit of unity, while allowing for variety in individual ministries as to their work, calling, and location as directed by the Holy Spirit (Acts 10:34,35; 1 Cor. 12:12-31).

<u>Blood Atonement:</u> We believe in the saving power of the blood of Jesus and His imputed righteousness (Acts 4:12; Rom. 4:1-9, 5:1-11; Eph. 1:3-14).

<u>Bodily Resurrection:</u> We believe in the bodily resurrection of Jesus Christ (Luke 24:39-43; John 20:24-29).

<u>Ascension:</u> We believe that Christ Jesus ascended to the Father and is presently engaged in building a place for us in His Kingdom and interceding for the saints (John 14:2,3; Rom. 8:34).

<u>Second Coming:</u> We believe in the visible, bodily return of Christ Jesus to this earth, to meet His Church (Bride) and to judge the world (Acts 1:10,11; 1 Thess. 4:13-18; 2 Thess. 1:7-10; James 5:8; Rev. 1:7).

<u>Ordinances:</u> We believe that the two ordinances of the Body of Christ are water baptism and the Lord's Supper (Matt. 28:19; 1 Cor.11:24-26).

<u>Heaven and Hell:</u> We believe Scripture clearly sets forth the doctrines of eternal punishment for the lost and eternal bliss and service for the saved — a literal hell for the unsaved and Heaven for the saved (Matt. 25:34,41,46; Luke 16:19-31; John 14:1-3; Rev. 20:11-15).

<u>Holy Spirit:</u> We believe the Holy Spirit to be the third person of the Trinity whose purpose in the redemption of man is to convict of sin, regenerate the repentant believer, guide the believer into all truth, indwell all believers, and give gifts to those He wills that they may minister as Christ would to men. We believe that the manifestations of the Holy Spirit recorded in 1 Corinthians 12:1-11 will operate through present-day Christians who yield to Jesus (Luke 11:13; John 7:37-39, 14:16,17, 16:7-14; Acts 2:1-18).

We believe the baptism in the Holy Spirit, with the evidence of speaking in other tongues as the Spirit gives utterance, is for all believers as promised by John the Baptist (Matt. 3:11), Jesus (Acts 1:4-8), and Peter (Acts 2:38-41). The fulfillment of this promise was witnessed by early disciples of Christ (Acts 2:4, 10:44-47, 19:1-6) and operates in many present-day disciples of the Lord Jesus Christ.

    <u>Divine Healing:</u> We believe God has used doctors, medicines, and other natural means as channels of healing; however, we believe divine healing is provided for believers in the atonement made by Jesus' blood shed on the cross (Isa. 53:5; 1 Pet. 2:24). We believe divine healing may be appropriated by the laying on of hands by the elders (James 5:14-16), by the prayer of an anointed person gifted by the Holy Spirit for healing the sick (1 Cor. 12:9), or by a direct act of receiving this provision by faith (Mark 11:23,24).

MINISTRY FINANCING

> But seek ye first the kingdom of God, and his righteousness; and all these things shall be added unto you.
>
> Matthew 6:33

    We want to share with readers the instructions the Lord gave us in regard to financing this ministry. As this is the Holy Spirit's work, we are to let Him speak to the hearts of people as to what and how much He wants them to give. Quite simply, we are to share the vision He has given us and trust Him to provide for all that we need. We believe the Lord pays for the things He orders, and if He does not order something, we do not want to engage in it. Pray with us that we will stay close to the Lord, and that, in seeking His righteousness, we will be able to hear His instructions clearly as to what He desires us to do. If we do that, we know we shall never lack of the things needed to do His work.

    CHRIST UNLIMITED MINISTRIES, INC. is a 501(c)(3) tax-exempt, non-profit, church established locally in the Dewey, Arizona, area.

[1]Barrett, David B. <u>Cosmos, Chaos, and Gospel</u> (Birmingham: New Hope Publishers, 1987), p. 75.

Christ Unlimited — P.O. Box 850 — Dewey, AZ 86327   USA

Exposing Satan's Devices Workbook

Answers to Lessons and Quizzes

Christ Unlimited — P.O. Box 850 — Dewey, AZ 86327   USA

Answers to Lesson, Section One

I. Satan's Name and Origin
  A.1.Adversary, enemy, accuser
    2.a. Abaddon   b. Accuser
      c. Adversary   d. Angel of Bottomless Pit
      e. Apollyon   f. The Prince of Devils
      g. Belial   h. Destroyer
      i. Devil   j. Enemy
      k. Liar/Father of Lies   l. Great Red Dragon
      m.Thief   n. Lucifer
      o. King of Tyrus   p. Murderer
      q. Old Serpent   r. Prince of This World
      s. Beelzebub   t. Prince of the Power of the Air
      u. Serpent   v. Spirit That Worketh in the
                                       Children of Disobedience

      w Tempter   x. God of This World
      y. The Wicked One   z. Robber and Thief
    aa. Antichrist   bb. Beast
  B. God created Satan.
    1. Cherub, or angelic being.
    2. Lucifer
    3. Free
    4. Rebel
    5. Pride
    6. Five
    7. To live independently of God's will, asserting his
       own will against God's, which is rebellion.
  C. Evil — good
    1. Good and perfect
    2. Satan and sin
    3. Choice
    4. Overcome
II. Recognizing Satan's Devices
  A. By studying God's Word
  B. No!
  C. Yes
  D.1. Ignorant
    2. Fear
    3. Blame God
    4. Power — power
    5. Deception

Christ Unlimited — P.O. Box 850 — Dewey, AZ 86327   USA

Answers to Review Outline Quiz, Section One

1. Satan and one-third of the angels in Heaven
2. The lake of fire
3. Luke 10:19,20; Mark 16:17,18; James 4:7, plus others
    that also apply
4. d,c,e,a,f,b
5. True
6. Pride, self-will, and rebellion
7a. Evil spirits
  b. Spirits of dead unbelievers
  c. Living unbelievers
  d. Backslidden Christians
8a. To distract us from reading the Bible
  b. Praying
  c. Fellowshipping
    with other believers
9. Through deception
10. Through the word of our testimony and the blood of Jesus

Christ Unlimited — P.O. Box 850 — Dewey, AZ 86327   USA

Answers to Lesson, Section Two

I. Satan Deceives Men
    A. Ignorant
    B. Chose
    C. Own Ways
    D. Reject or deny

II. Satan's Deceptive Methods
    A. Laws, instructions, or Word (Any or all of these is correct.)
    B. Doubt
    C. Tempt
    D. Self
    E. Will of God
    F. Pride
        1a. An overly high opinion of oneself; haughtiness,
            arrogance
        1b. Dignity and self-respect or self-esteem
        2. Beauty
        3. Lust
        4. Arrogance in regard to the gifts, graces, talents,
           ministries, and abilities bestowed on a person by God
        5. Destruction and a fall
    G. 1. Lust of the eyes
       2. Lust of the flesh
       3. Pride of life
       4. Love;world
    H. Wolves
       1. Victims
       2. Escape
    I. Hastily or rashly
       1. Gentle and patient
       2. The enemy (or Satan, or the devil)
       3. Peace and rest
    J. Religions and gods
       1. Anything a person considers the most important thing
          in his life, whose power he thinks is the greatest,
          and whose favor he would do anything or give anything
          to win.
       2. Idol
       3a. A "concrete" thing, made of literal earthly materials
        b. A mythical character
        c. A mental idea
       4a. Drink or other addictive substances

        b. Pleasure — food, hobbies, sex
        c. Money and/or material possessions
        d. Power
        e. Other people
        f. Themselves
        g. Man-made objects
           (Answers do not have to be exactly the same, nor in
           the same order, but should convey the same thought.)
    5. The God of the Bible, the Creator of the Universe

III. False Religions
    A. The atoning blood of Jesus
    B. Jesus' Second Coming to earth
    C. A literal fiery hell that is eternal
    D. The one way to Heaven is through Jesus Christ alone

IV. Cultic Religions
    A. 1. Any form of religious worship; a sect
       2. A group that deviates from basic Bible doctrines
    B. Threads, or portions
    C. The Word of God
    D. Error
    E. To fulfill a legitimate hunger in the human spirit
    F. The Lord, God, Christ, or Jesus (Any one is correct.)
    G. Path or way
    H. Relationship
    I. Renounce those things and seek God

Christ Unlimited — P.O. Box 850 — Dewey, AZ 86327   USA

Answers to Review Outline Quiz, Section Two

1. Rob, steal, kill, and destroy
2. To tempt, worry, and cause anxiety
3. A demon masquerading as the Holy Spirit, operating in false supernatural manifestations, false gifts of the Spirit, and false doctrines
4. Idolatry
5. Worshipping, or putting ahead of God anything or anyone
6a. If their beliefs deviate from the doctrines of the faith (Heb. 6:1,2)
  b. If they do not teach the atoning blood of Jesus
  c. If they do not believe in the literal second coming of Christ
  d. If they do not believe in a literal Heaven and Hell
  e. If they do not teach there is only one way to eternal life with God the Father: Jesus Christ
      (Any three of the five above are correct).
7. Confuse, alienate, or ensnare believers
8. The believer
9. The Word of God
10. Counterfeits

Christ Unlimited — P.O. Box 850 — Dewey, AZ 86327   USA

Answers to Lesson, Section Three

I. Satan's Religions: The Occult
    A. Counterfeiting
    B. "Secret" or "hidden"
    C. Doctrines of devils
    D. Influence and control
    E. Idolatry
    F. Curse
    G. Divination, observer of times, consulter with familiar
       spirits, marking the skin (tattoos), "curious arts,"
       plus others
    H. ESP, transcendental meditation, horoscopes, plus others
       (See the list of occult practices, page 21 in Exposing
       Satan's Devices.)
    I. 1. Savior
        2a. Divine
         b. Human
         c. Virgin
         d. Blood
         e. Resurrected
         f. Bodily
         g. Son of God
         h. Alive

    J. 1. The ideal truth
        2. The divine idea
        3. The greatest personage
        4. The chief agent of life
        5. The glorious spirit creature
        6. The unity of all mankind

II. Cultic Religions' Views of Hell
    A.
        1. Fear
        2. Altogether, or completely
        3. Hereafter
        4. Soul sleep, or rest
        5. Permanent
        6. Annihilated
        7. "Second chance"
        8. Separation

B.
1. Devil and his angels
2. Worm — quenched
3. Hades — Sheol
4. Grave
   a. "The pit"
   b. "The place of the dead"
   c. "The deep"
5. Gates and bars
6. Judgment
7.
   a. Shame
   b. Remorse
   c. Full memory
   d. Full consciousness
   e. Anguish
   f. Torment
8. Paradise
   a. A great gulf
   b. Abraham's Bosom
   c. Resurrection
      1) "Captivity captive"
      2) Delivered
   d. Gates of Hell
   e. Heaven
   f. Death and Hell
      1) Lake of fire
      2) Death

III. Marks of Cults
   A. Treasures
      1.
         a. Physically, through finances
         b. Emotionally (or mentally)
         c. Spiritually
      2. Authority
   B. Secret revelations
   C. Doctrinal
      1. Portion
      2. Believe
   D. Spirit, Soul, and Body
   E. Legalism

IV. God's Leadership Versus Satan's Control
    A. Love and respect
    B. Fear and false promises

Answers to Review Outline Quiz, Section Three

1. There is only one path to Heaven: Jesus Christ.
2. We know there is a Hell because the Bible tells us so.
3. Astrology, divination, witchcraft, fortune telling, and so forth.
4. Demons who pretend to be spirits of dead people.
5. People who allow demons to use them as a "medium" to bring others alleged messages from dead relatives or famous people.
6. Stars, idols
7. The gifts of God and the Holy Spirit
8. Love and pray
9. Counterfeits
10. Evil and curses

Answers to Lesson, Section Four

I. Demons Inhabit Cultic and Occultic Objects
    A. 1a. Statues of pagan gods (such as Buddha)
        b. Masks from foreign lands
        c. Obsessive collecting of animal figures
           (Answers could be Confucius paintings, voodoo dolls,
           or similar objects.)
      2a. Kachina dolls
        b. Yeibichai designs on rugs
        c. Indian "god's eyes" made with yarn
           (Answers could be other such objects, particularly the
           "Thunderbird," totem poles, squash blossoms, and other
           idolatrous art forms.)

    B. 1. Dowsing sticks, or "water wands"
       2. Ouija boards
       3. Ankh, unicorn horn, mood rings, and Star of David
           (The answer could be any of these.)
       4. Rock
         a. Country/western music
         b. Jazz
         c. Popular
      5a. "I Dream of Jeannie"
        b. "Star Wars"
        c. "Bewitched"
        d. "The Gremlins"
        e. "Doom"
    (Again, the answers could have been other such programs and
    films and be correct; for example, all of the "Friday the
    13th" films are evil.)
       6. Destroyed
      7a. "That frightens me to death!"
        b. "I could kill her (or him)."
        c. "Cross my fingers"
        d. "He has strong vibes."
        e. "If my luck holds out."

II. How Can We Overcome the Powers of Darkness?
    A. Destroy the objects by smashing or burning.
    B. Repent of the sin of being involved with witchcraft.
    C. Cast the spirits behind the objects out of the house.
    D. Invite the Holy Spirit to cleanse us.
III. Can Demons Dwell in Christians?

Christ Unlimited — P.O. Box 850 — Dewey, AZ 86327   USA

A. Demons are spirit beings invisible to us.

B. They walk, hear, speak, see, obey, seek, think, know, and dwell in human or animal bodies whenever possible.

C. 1. Their master, Satan

   2. The Godhead — Father, Son, and Holy Spirit

   3. Believers through the name of Jesus and the power of the Holy Spirit

D. 1. Seeing demons in everyone and everything

   2. Ignoring the devil and refusing to believe a Christian can have a demon

E. 1. The flesh itself

   2. Evil spirits that fasten themselves to some aspect of the flesh

F. Crucifying

G. Children

H. 1. Enslavement

   2. Defilement

   3. Torment

I. Deliverance

   1. Common

   2a. Peter

    b. Paul

   (Philip also is a correct answer.)

J. Cast out

   1. Discerning of spirits

   2. Infirmity

K. No

   1. Territory

   2. Captives

   3. Oppressing — possessing

   4. Degree

    a. Filled

    b. Gadarene demoniac

    c. To display their destructive power

    d. One

    e. The insane, suicidal, and those with obvious mental problems

L. 1. Being born again

   2. Making a verbal confession of faith in Jesus

   3. Repenting and confessing the sin that gave a demon or demons access to his life

   4. Renouncing each lie the devil used to cause him to sin, and replacing it with the truth of God's Word

   5. Resisting the devil and commanding demons to flee

M. Born-again, Spirit-filled Christians, praying in faith

Christ Unlimited — P.O. Box 850 — Dewey, AZ 86327   USA

Answers to Review Outline Quiz, Section Four

1. False
2a. To avoid fellowship with darkness
   b. To avoid negative or ungodly speech
   c. To seek to be a "light" to those around us
3a. Sin
   b. Disobedience to God
   c. Lack of knowledge
4. Any verse of Psalm 91, plus many other promises in the Word
5a. From ancestral "chains of iniquities" (Exodus 20:4,5)
5b. Repent of sins and receive Jesus as Savior, also break any "chains of iniquity" through prayer and obedience to God (Exodus 20:6; Acts 5:29-32).
6. Evil — good
7. Ungodly practices or associations, altered states of consciousness and other New Age practices and teachings, or generational curses (Any one of these is a correct answer.)
8. Through the shedding of His blood and His death on the cross
9. Through emotional, mental, or physical illnesses
10. The Kingdom of God

Answers to Lesson, Section Five

I. Guidelines for casting out demons.
    A. Born-again, Spirit-filled Christians
        1. Faith
        2. Fear
        3. Through the name of Jesus, we have authority over them.
    B. Faith
    C. Without Jesus, the demons have authority over you.
        1. They were beaten, had their clothes torn off, and fled
            down the street naked and wounded.
        2. They were not born-again believers.

II. Methods of casting out demons
    A. Holy Spirit
    B. As the Spirit shows you through discernment
    C. As the Spirit leads. However, understand the importance of the
       blood of Jesus, but do not treat the blood as an object. Jesus
       should be the focus.
    D. No; we should command them not to speak.
    E. 1. Seek another habitat
       2. Wander in dry places
       3. Go back to Hades
    F. No, only their influence can be removed or destroyed.
    G. We must cooperate with God and use the authority we have
       given over Satan by Jesus.
    H. Filled

III. Manifestations and Symptoms of Demononic Oppression
    A. 1. Crying   4. Screaming
       2. Falling down as dead 5. Wallowing on the floor
       3. Foaming at the mouth 6. Vomiting

    B. 1. Unreasonable   4. Abnormal
       2. Tormenting   5. Uncontrollable
       3. Enslaving   6. Addicting

    C. (Answers do not have to be in this order):
       1. Unclean or foul spirits   6. Seducing spirits
       2. Perverse spirits   7. Spirits of slumber
       3. Sorrowful spirits   8. Spirits of jealousy
       4. Anti-Christ spirits   9. Spirits of whoredom
       5. Spirits of bondage   10. Spirit of devils

Christ Unlimited — P.O. Box 850 — Dewey, AZ 86327   USA

(Other spirits you could have named include: spirits of error, dumb spirits, spirits of divination, familiar spirits, and spirits of fear.)

D. 1. Fear 　　5. Depression 　　9. Anxiety 　　　13. Loneliness
　　2. Hate 　　6. Self-pity 　　　10. Rejection 　　14. Resentment
　　3. Pride 　　7. Rebellion 　　　11. Jealousy 　　15. Impatience
　　4. Envy 　　8. Lust 　　　　　12. Doubt 　　　16. Greed

(Also any area mentioned in **Galatians 5:19-21**)

E. 1. Tumors 　　　5. Cancers 　　　9. Crippling diseases
　　2. Arthritis 　　6. Blindness 　　10. Ulcers
　　3. Hayfever 　　7. Asthma 　　　11. Allergies
　　4. Epilepsy 　　8. Fevers 　　　12. Heart problems

F. Seducing — whoredoms
　　1. Religious
　　2. Counterfeit
　　3a. Weird sights, sounds, and smells
　　3b. Visitations

IV. Concerning Curses
　　A. A curse that comes down on the children because of a forefather's sins
　　B. Obeyed and walked
　　C. Only if that person is in sin, disobedience, or out of the will of God
　　　　1. An evil word spoken against someone
　　　　2. A good word spoken over someone
　　D. 1. Stray from or forsake
　　　　2. Are immature
　　　　3. Are unstable
　　E. Indirectly
　　F. Love and obey
　　G. Prayer and forgiveness toward those who curse us
　　H. Overcome evil with good

Christ Unlimited — P.O. Box 850 — Dewey, AZ 86327   USA

Answers to Review Outline Quiz, Section Five

1. Spirit-filled believers who are walking in faith
2. The Great Commission (Mark 16:15-18)
3. Crying, screaming, vomiting, wallowing on the floor
4. No, the person doing the deliverance can find out its name through the gift of discernment by the Holy Spirit, if he needs to know.
5. Evil words spoken against someone
6. Cancer or other tormenting diseases
7. No
8. You must renounce sin and receive the blessings in faith.
9. Negative words
10. Through repentance and renouncing sin, prayer, faith in God's Word, and by overcoming evil with good

Answers to Lesson, Section Six

I. Warfare Against the Devil:
   A. Spiritual ignorance or ignorance of God's word
   B. Spiritual laws and spiritual warfare
   C. Jesus defeated the works of Satan by his death and resurrection and delegated the authority of His Kingdom to His Body, Christians, so we now have power over Satan, his works, and his demons.
   D. Battle or Warfare
   E. Army of God

II. Concerning Spiritual Warfare
   A. By first putting on the armor of God, the armor of light
   B. The mind
      1. Spirit
      2. God's Word
      3. Recognize
      4. Heart
      5. Suggestion
   C. Traditions and doctrines of men
   D. Resist
      1. Evil spirits (or demons)
      2. Rebuked
      3. Holy Spirit
      4. He prayed for him
      5. Strife or evil

III. The Christian's Weapons and Warfare
   A. 1.
      a. Having our minds renewed from the world
      b. Guard our minds with the Word of God
      2. a. To be in right-standing
      b. No
      c. God
         1) Condemnation
         2) Righteous
      3. Gospel of Peace
      a. Peace
      b. Peacemakers
      4. The Shield of Faith

Christ Unlimited — P.O. Box 850 — Dewey, AZ 86327   USA

       a. Faith

       b. Sin

  5. a. Thinking or having

       b. Imagination

  6. The Sword of the Spirit, or the Word of God

       a. Offensive

       b. Overcomers

       c. Speaking

B. The full armor of God

  1. Always, or continuously

       a. 1) Praying in the Spirit or Tounges

          2) Praying with the understanding (one's native tongue)

       b. Tongues

  2. Loud, or noisy

       a. Wisdom

       b. Persistent, or unceasing

       c. Disciplined

  3. Light

Christ Unlimited — P.O. Box 850 — Dewey, AZ 86327   USA

Answers to Review Outline Quiz, Section Six

1. Six
2. a. Helmet of salvation
   b. Breastplate of righteousness
   c. Belt of truth
   d. "Sandals" of gospel of peace
   e. Shield of faith
   f. Sword of the Spirit, or the Word of God
3. Luke 10:19,20; Mark 16:17,18; James 4:7, as well as others.
4. The first five listed in Ephesians 6:11-18
5. The Sword of the Spirit
6a. Prayer, including the prayer of agreement
   b. Fasting
   c. The name of Jesus
   d. Warring in the Spirit
7. Satan and his demons
8. Heaven and hell
9. Submit unto God.
10 a. Praying in the natural
   b. Praying in the Spirit (tongues)

Christ Unlimited — P.O. Box 850 — Dewey, AZ 86327   USA

FOR ADDITIONAL STUDY

This book is taken from a course of Bible studies called the Overcoming Life Series. The entire series is a virtual "spiritual tool chest," as it covers a multitude of subjects every Christian faces in his walk with God. It also answers questions that many believers have concerning the current move of God. These are dealt with in a balanced approach and in the light of the Scripture. God's people are not to live frustrated, defeated lives, but rather they are to be victorious overcomers! Other books available with their companion workbooks are:

PROVE ALL THINGS - Christ warned that great deception would be one of the signs of the end times. In this book, instruction is given on how to recognize false prophets and teachings. Clear Scriptural guidelines are given on discerning the Spirit of truth versus the spirit of error. The book deals with how to judge without being judgmental.

THE TRUE GOD - This is a teaching on the character of God, explaining why God does certain things, and why it is against His nature to do other things. It differentiates between the things for which God is responsible and the things for which the devil is responsible. Our responsibility as Christians destined to overcome is made clear so that we can live victorious lives.

THE WILL OF GOD - This lesson teaches us not only how to know the will of God in our personal lives, family, ministry and finances, but also brings understanding as to why God allows sin, sickness and suffering in the world. As overcomers, Christians are not to suffer under many of the things we have accepted as normal.

KEYS TO THE KINGDOM - Instruction on how to gain authority in God's Kingdom through prayer is the topic of this book. Many principles and methods of prayer are covered, such as praying in the Spirit, fasting and prayer, travailing prayer, praise, intercession and spiritual warfare.

EXPOSING SATAN'S DEVICES - This book is a powerful expose' of Satan's tricks, tactics and lies. Cult and Occultic methods and groups are listed so Christians can detect their activity. Demon activity is discussed and deliverance and casting out demons is dealt with in detail. Satan's kingdom is uncovered and the Christian is taught to overcome through spiritual discernment and warfare.

HEALING OF THE SPIRIT, SOUL AND BODY -This book teaches how to overcome emotional problems, as well as physical ones, and how to receive divine healing. It also teaches how to renew the carnal mind and walk in the spirit of life, thereby overcoming depression, loneliness and fear.

NEITHER MALE NOR FEMALE -What is the woman's role in the church and home? Who is a woman's spiritual head and covering? Does God call women to the five-fold ministry? What does God's Word say about divorce, celibacy and choosing a marriage partner? These and other woman related topics are Scripturally examined.

EXTREMES OR BALANCE? -Many Christians have hurt the cause of Christ through "out-of-balance" teachings and demonstrations. This book shows how to avoid those areas. It also deals wisely with the excesses and extremes in the body of Christ.

THE PATHWAY INTO THE OVERCOMER'S WALK - This book contains answers to the questions an overcomer faces as he presses toward the prize of the high calling in Christ Jesus. How can we be conformed to the image of Christ? How does the Holy Spirit work with the overcomers in the end times? What are the overcomer's rewards?

Please visit our website for information on how to order the complete "Overcoming Life Series." BibleResource.org is also an excellent source for additional Bible resources.

www.BibleResources.org

Christ Unlimited — P.O. Box 850 — Dewey, AZ 86327   USA